creative
techniques *for*
polymer clay
jewelry

nanetta **bananto**

North Light Books
Cincinnati, Ohio
www.artistsnetwork.com

09 08 07 06 05   5 4 3 2 1

Library of Congress Cataloging-in-Publication Data

Bananto, Nanetta

    Creative techniques for polymer clay jewelry / Nanetta Bananto.

        p. cm.

    ISBN 1-58180-651-5

    1. Polymer clay craft. 2. Jewelry making. I. Title.

    TT297.B36 2005

    745.594'2--dc22

                                    2004061749

EDITOR: Krista Hamilton

DESIGNER: Leigh Ann Lentz

LAYOUT ARTIST: Donna Cozatchy

PRODUCTION COORDINATOR: Robin Richie

PHOTOGRAPHERS: Hal Barkan, Sylvia Bissonnette, Al Parrish, and Christine Polomsky

PHOTOGRAPHY STYLIST: Nora Martini

AUTHOR PHOTOGRAPH: Nanetta Bananto

About the Author

Nanetta Bananto designs original art in her Augusta, Kansas, studio. Although she works in a variety of media, including beadwork, paper, ink, precious metal clay and fiber, her primary medium is polymer clay, which she has used for over twenty years. Nanetta has utilized this versatile material for one-of-a-kind dolls, candleholders, sculptures, jewelry and beads. Nanetta has been involved in art all her life and continues to experiment, evolve, teach, learn, share, acknowledge and inspire.

Metric Conversion Chart

To convert	to	multiply by
Inches	Centimeters	2.54
Centimeters	Inches	0.4
Feet	Centimeters	30.5
Centimeters	Feet	0.03
Yards	Meters	0.9
Meters	Yards	1.1
Sq. Inches	Sq. Centimeters	6.45
Sq. Centimeters	Sq. Inches	0.16
Sq. Feet	Sq. Meters	0.09
Sq. Meters	Sq. Feet	10.8
Sq. Yards	Sq. Meters	0.8
Sq. Meters	Sq. Yards	1.2
Pounds	Kilograms	0.45
Kilograms	Pounds	2.2
Ounces	Grams	28.4
Grams	Ounces	0.04

Dedication

This book is dedicated to my family and friends who have supported and encouraged me through many years, enabling me to follow the path which has led me to these pages; and to my husband, Mark Horton, who lifts me up and brings me down to earth as needed.

Acknowledgments

A special thank you to the following people who have contributed to completion of this book:

Jan Walcott, from Polyform Products, for letting me get my feet wet by writing projects, and for generously supplying all the clay needed for this book. Skippy Sanches, for your time, talent, commitment and great stories. Nick Bananto, Niall, Elliot and Mark Horton, for softening clay, moving equipment, lifting boxes and helping me when I asked. Tricia Waddell, for opening the door and giving me a chance. Krista Hamilton, for your patience, professionalism and for being the best editor a first time author could ask for. Christine Doyle, for working out the kinks. Christine Polomsky, for the ease with which you use the studio and the beautiful results. All the designers and photographers at North Light Books who lent their talents to this publication.

Contents

INTRODUCTION

After twenty years of working with polymer clay, I continue to be amazed at its versatility. It is a material that can be used by children and adults; it is easily obtained, worked and baked; it is therapeutic; it has a long shelf life; and it leaves no waste. Working with polymer clay is an exercise in color, form and possibility!

Although I work with this medium almost daily, I find there is always something new to learn. The rules are as malleable as the clay. Granted, the rules of safety are rigid and should never be overlooked, but all else is left to your own interpretation.

I have learned a lot about polymer clay by looking, listening, reading and experimenting. The polymer clay community is vast, and I acknowledge that community as a great inspiration. One has only to open a book, turn on the television or browse the Internet to feel the open arms of those working in this medium. Indeed, there is always something innovative on the horizon, and the fact that there are so many polymer clay enthusiasts willing to share ideas and techniques makes polymer clay an ever-evolving art that welcomes anyone interested.

When I am working on a new piece of polymer clay jewelry, I first go through the basics of conditioning my clay and choosing my color combinations. Then I roll or stack the clay into canes. My workspace is cluttered with canes that combine like confetti in a kaleidoscope. My designs are never rigidly planned. Once my canes

are designed, then I make my jewelry. It seems only appropriate that I set the book up in the same manner in which I work, therefore I have divided it into three sections: Getting Started, Canes and Projects.

The Getting Started section includes a glossary of terms, tools and materials, polymer clay basics and polymer clay techniques. You will also find recipes for how to create any of the projects in the book in ten different color palettes.

The Canes section features detailed instructions for making fifteen easy and beautiful canes. You can apply what you have learned here to make any of the pendants, bracelets, pins and earrings in the Projects section. This is where you'll find twenty step-by-step projects and twenty-two variations, each designed in one of the ten color palettes.

As you create the jewelry pieces in this book, feel free to try different color combinations, create matching sets or make several to give as gifts. Once you have the basics under your belt, the sky is the limit. Experiment, modify, discover—take my ideas and make them your own. If you think of the process as the goal, there will always be new life in your polymer clay endeavors.

GETTING STARTED

This section will give you an overall introduction to polymer clay. First, you'll need to familiarize yourself with the basic "language" of polymer clay, which I use throughout the book. Some of the words may already be familiar to you, and others may be quite new. Refer back to the glossary from time to time if you need to refresh your memory.

Next, you'll need to get acquainted with the tools and materials required for the projects in this book. One of the best things about working with polymer clay is the minimal amount of essential tools and supplies. Besides a few special items and the clay itself, you'll find most of what you need lying around the house! But you may still want to take a trip to the craft and hardware stores to browse for a few must-have items that you don't already have on hand.

Once you've mastered the language and collected your tools, you'll need to know some basic information about this fun and flexible medium. I have included a brief explanation of polymer clay, as well as instructions for conditioning, mixing, blending, transferring images, baking, storing and more.

When you have completed this section, you will have a strong foundation in polymer clay and will be ready to move on to the next section. In no time at all, you will be creating one-of-a-kind jewelry that will beautify your wardrobe and dazzle your family and friends.

Glossary

Throughout the book—and in the polymer clay community in general—there are a number of terms that are used to describe the medium. I have listed a few of the most important ones.

ANTIQUE: to artificially simulate age and wear by applying a dark paint, then wiping it off with a soft cloth. (For an example, see the Goddess Pendant on page 48.)

BATIK: a fabric-decorating artform in which parts of the fabric are covered in hot wax, the exposed fabric is dyed, and then the wax is removed to reveal a design. (For an example of faux batik, see the Tribal Choker on page 80.)

BURNISH: to rub a tool such as a bone folder or the back of a spoon on a surface in a circular motion to smooth the surface or to adhere or transfer an object or image.

CANE: a roll, block, stack or log of clay, inside which a design runs lengthwise. When the cane is sliced, the design is exposed. Canes can be reduced or enlarged to get the same design or pattern in various sizes.

CLOISONNÉ: an enameling technique in which colored glass is separated by thin strips of metal. (The Butterfly Pin on page 52 mimics this technique.)

COLLAGE: a technique that ties several elements together to make an artistic piece. (For an example, see the Fragment Pin on page 116.)

CONDITION: to make clay soft and pliable by kneading, warming and rolling it through a pasta machine. (For instructions, see page 15.)

CURE: to bake clay so that it sets permanently and is no longer soft or workable. (For instructions, see page 16.)

CYANOACRYLATE: a strong, quick-setting adhesive, also known as superglue.

DESIGN SHEET: a sheet of raw polymer clay that has been decorated with various canes and embellishments.

FAUX: an imitation of a real material, such as marble, or technique, such as batik.

FINISH: to sand, buff and polish baked clay with wet/dry sandpaper, a soft cloth or a muslin wheel. (For instructions, see page 16.)

IMAGE TRANSFER: the process of imprinting a photocopied image into polymer clay. (For instructions, see page 21.)

INCLUSION: anything that can be mixed into clay, such as metal leaf, glitter, embossing powder or spices, to change the color or add a decorative element.

KNEAD: to work clay with your hands by stretching, pulling and warming.

LEACH: to remove plasticizer from sticky clay by placing it on a piece of clean white paper. The plasticizer will seep into the paper and the clay will become stiffer.

MILLEFIORE: a technique, literally meaning "a thousand flowers," from which canes were derived. It is often seen in Venetian glass, where a pattern runs throughout the length of a piece.

MOKUME GANE: a technique derived from Japanese metal working that involves stacking layers of clay, manipulating the clay by cutting and shaping, then slicing thin layers off the top to reveal rings of the different layers. (For an example, see the mokume gane cane on page 38.)

MOSAIC: a design formed from many small colored tiles. (For an example, see the Mermaid Pin on page 60.)

PLASTICIZER: a chemical in plastic that makes it softer and more flexible. Too much may cause clay to have a sticky consistency.

REDUCE: to make the diameter of a cane thinner by rolling, stretching and pulling.

RELEASE AGENT: any substance, such as water or baby powder, that keeps clay and other objects from sticking together.

SCORE: to make short, shallow cuts in a smooth surface to help it grab adhesives and as an antiquing effect, as shown in the Asian Pendant on page 98.

SKINNER BLEND: a technique developed by Judith Skinner for creating smooth gradations of color on one sheet of clay. (For instructions, see page 19.)

SNAKE: a long thin rope of clay.

TRANSLUCENT: a quality in clay and other objects which allows light to pass through. The thinner the object, the more translucent the effect.

WET SAND: to sand polymer clay to a smooth finish with wet/dry sandpaper by dipping it in water; cuts down on dust when sanding baked clay. (For instructions, see page 16.)

Clay can be rolled through a hand-cranked pasta machine like the one shown above to further condition it and to roll it into sheets in various thicknesses.

Pasta Machine

This machine, available in hand-cranked and motorized versions, makes conditioning, blending and rolling clay a whole lot easier. Rolling clay through the machine will result in a sheet with a consistent thickness. Pasta machines can be found in cook stores, craft stores and on the Internet. (For more information about using a pasta machine, see page 15.)

Adhesives

I use several types of adhesives for different purposes. Always follow the safety precautions on the package.

CRAFT GLUE: This white glue, which dries clear, works well for sticking raw clay to itself or to paper. Delta Sobo Craft and Fabric Glue and Aleene's Quick Dry Tacky Glue are my favorite brands.

JEWELRY ADHESIVE: This glue, which does not become brittle over time, is used for adhering jewelry findings, such as pinbacks, to baked clay. I like E6000 brand, which is strong and durable.

REVERSE COLLAGE GLUE: This specialty glue was designed for sticking papers and fabric to glass or plastic in mosaic projects. Aleene's Reverse Collage Glue is my favorite brand for gluing paper images to raw clay.

SUPERGLUE: Also called cyanoacrylate, this instant-bond glue is used for gluing findings and cords to jewelry pieces.

Sobo, Aleene's and E6000 are three high-quality adhesive brands that can be found in general craft stores.

On the next few pages, you will find a list of the tools needed for the projects in this book. You may already have some of these items on hand. There really are no "rules" for what you can and cannot use to shape, pierce, texture and decorate clay. Use your imagination, and you never know what tools you will invent to make your pieces unique!

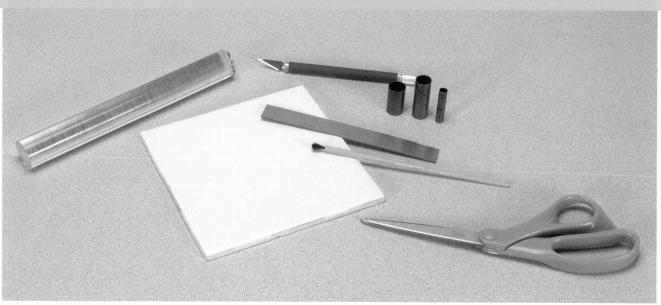

The tools shown above are used to cut, shape and pierce polymer clay. Clockwise from top left: acrylic roller, craft knife, circle cutters, tissue blade, craft paintbrush with plastic handle, ceramic tile and craft scissors.

Cutting, Shaping, Piercing and Baking

By using these tools to cut, pierce and shape your clay, it can take on any shape and texture you desire.

ACRYLIC ROLLER: This smooth acrylic rod, found in craft stores, is designed specifically for use with polymer clay. Wooden rolling pins leave a wood-grain texture in the clay, so use a smooth, straight glass bud vase if you don't have an acrylic roller.

ALUMINUM FOIL: This is used to shape clay and as a propping material. Heavy-duty cooking foil is easiest to work with. (For an example, see the Wearable Vessel on page 88.)

BONE FOLDER: I use this tool, which is made of bone, for smoothing, burnishing and transferring images onto clay. If you do not have a bone folder, the back of a spoon will work.

CARDSTOCK, TYPING PAPER AND INDEX CARDS: Plain white paper or cardstock can be used to keep raw clay from sticking to the baking surface, and prevents shiny spots when baking flat pieces. It can also be used to leach some of the plasticizer out of clay to make it stiffer.

CERAMIC TILE: Smooth, glazed ceramic tiles like those seen in kitchens and baths are great work surfaces for raw clay and are also excellent for baking flat pieces.

CRAFT KNIFE: This knife consists of a sharp, replaceable blade and a pencil-like holder. It is used for cutting and shaping polymer clay. X-acto is a popular brand.

DOWEL: This is a long, thin wooden stick similar to a pencil that can be used to make channels in clay bead trays. (For instructions, see page 23.)

EXAM GLOVES: Regular exam gloves, which are sold in craft and home improvement stores, are great for handling clay without transferring your fingerprints.

NEEDLE: A fine sewing or beading needle is used for piercing air bubbles in the surface of clay.

PAINTBRUSH: Disposable craft brushes with plastic handles are best to use with liquid polymer clay and water-based oil paints because they don't leave bristles behind and they are inexpensive enough to throw away after each use. The handles are also great for poking holes in raw clay. (For an example, see the mokume gane cane on page 38.)

SKEWER: Metal and bamboo skewers are great for making channels and drilling holes in the surface of clay.

SCISSORS: A pair of sharp scissors are useful for cutting out the templates and transfer images on pages 124–125.

SHAPE CUTTERS: Cutters come in various shapes and sizes and are used to cut and punch holes in raw clay. (For an example, see the Scrap Clay Earrings on page 118.)

TEXTURE SHEETS: These are sheets with different textures that can be pressed into the clay. They are available from several distributors, including Polyform. (For an example, see the Fragment Pin on page 116.)

TISSUE BLADE: This sharp, flexible blade allows you to make straight or curved slices into your clay.

TOASTER OVEN: This is a worthwhile investment when baking polymer clay. It is more economical to use and can be dedicated to polymer clay to avoid baking in the same oven where you bake food. (For safety information, see page 17.)

Embellishments

Here are just a few of the many embellishments you can use to decorate your polymer clay jewelry.

ACCENT BEADS: Beads made of glass, wood, metal or ceramic are great for accenting a jewelry piece. I use E beads, which are 4mm beads available in every color, for several projects in the book. You can also make your own beads from scrap clay. (For instructions, see page 22.)

COLORED PENCILS: These are great for coloring in images on baked clay. I use Prismacolor pencils, which are thick, soft and smooth. (For an example, see the Asian Pendant on page 98.)

EMBOSSING POWDER: This is a fine pigment powder that I used as a surface accent in the Wearable Vessel project on page 88. It can also be heated, which causes the powder to melt into a liquid form.

GLITTER: Apply this to raw polymer clay and bake to create a shiny effect. (For an example, see the Bamboo Pin on page 84.)

METAL LEAF: This is an extremely thin, delicate sheet of metal that can be applied to a surface. It is available in gold, silver, copper and variegated. (For an example, see the Crackle Pin on page 76.)

METALLIC WAX: I use a wax-based paste by Treasure Gold to highlight finished pieces. It is applied with a soft cloth to add highlights and bring out the texture. (For an example, see the Egyptian Princess Pin on page 104.)

NAIL POLISH REMOVER: Acetone-based nail polish remover is used for making photocopy transfers. It reacts with and melts the toner of the photocopy, causing the image to bond with the clay. (For instructions, see page 21.)

WATER-BASED OIL PAINT: This type of paint seeps into the surface of polymer clay, giving it a waxy, deep antique finish. It is easily thinned and cleans up with water. I use a brand called Grumbacher Max. (For an example, see the Goddess Pendant on page 48.)

WET/DRY SANDPAPER: Sandpaper that can be used with water is essential for sanding polymer clay pieces to a smooth finish. It sands more efficiently and prevents you from inhaling clay dust. (For instructions, see page 16.)

Embellishments such as the ones shown here will make your jewelry unique. Left to right: nail polish remover, assorted beads, embossing powder, sandpaper and colored pencils.

Jewelry Tools and Findings

You don't have to search high and low for these jewelry tools and findings. Your local craft stores should carry them, or you may already have them at home.

EARRING FINDINGS: These metal fasteners complete earrings. Several styles are available, including posts that glue directly onto the backs of the baked clay pieces and French earring wires that allow the earrings to dangle.

EYEPIN: This is a metal pin with a loop, or eye, at one end. It is used to make earring stems, pendants and dangle loops.

HEADPIN: This metal pin is similar to an eyepin, but instead of an eye, it has a tiny flat head at one end. It is used to make earring stems, pendants and dangle loops. Both eyepins and headpins can be made, but for the purposes of this book, I used purchased ones, which are available in craft and jewelry stores.

JEWELRY CORD AND WIRE: This is used for making necklaces on which pendants hang. It is available in many styles and materials, including nylon, elastic, leather and memory wire, which snaps back into shape when expanded and released.

JUMP RING: This metal ring connects jewelry loops, dangles and findings together. It can be opened and closed with pliers.

PINBACK: This is a metal pin bar that is glued to the back of a pin. It usually contains holes for grabbing the glue.

PLIERS: I highly recommend investing in a pair of rosary pliers, which is a combination of round-nose pliers and wire cutters. The ends can be used for looping, twisting and bending wire, while the cutter can be used for trimming wire. Needle-nose pliers are also helpful for opening and closing jump rings.

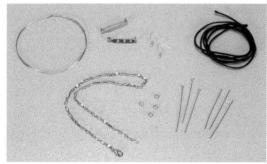

Jewelry findings such as these can be purchased in specialty jewelry stores and many craft stores. Clockwise from top left: memory wire, pinbacks, French earring hooks, nylon cord, headpins, eyepins, jump rings and chain.

In order to have a safe and enjoyable experience creating polymer clay jewelry, it is important to understand the basics of the medium. In this section, you will learn what polymer clay is, as well as how to condition, bake, finish and store it safely and effectively.

Understanding Polymer Clay

Polymer clay is basically plastic in an uncured state. It is made of polyvinyl chloride (PVC), pigment, filler and plasticizer. Different manufacturers use different combinations of these substances, which gives each brand its distinct qualities.

Polymer clay is manufactured in several countries under various brand names. Premo is a strong but flexible clay that is very durable after baking. It requires minimal conditioning to be workable and is available in a wide selection of colors, including metallics. Sculpey III is the softest and most economical polymer clay, and it requires very little conditioning to be pliable. Try mixing it with translucent Premo to make it stronger. Fimo is a strong, stiff clay. This makes it great for caning, but it requires considerable conditioning before use. Amazing Eraser Clay can be sculpted into a usable eraser, as it becomes very flexible after baking. It can also be used to make your own texture sheets. Cernit and Kato Polyclay are two other popular brands that are readily available. Each artist has a preference based on his or her individual needs.

Liquid polymer clay is literally that—a liquid form of polymer clay. It is available in opaque white and translucent. It can be painted onto the surface of raw or baked clay, layered and tinted with dry pigments or oil paint. Alone, it will become a flexible sheet that can be trimmed with scissors after baking. As a glaze, it can be applied over polymer clay, paper and even fabric. It can also be used as an adhesive or repair medium for your polymer clay pieces. My liquid polymer clay of choice is Translucent Liquid Sculpey (TLS), which has a semi-transparent appearance when baked.

Choosing a Work Surface

When working with polymer clay, choose a surface that will give you plenty of space to work freely. It should be smooth, and you should be able to cut on it. For demonstration purposes, I will be working on a craft table for the projects in this book. I recommend, however, that you work on a smooth ceramic tile. Ceramic tiles are available in sizes up to 18" x 18" (45.7cm x 45.7cm).

Do not mold or leave your clay sitting on surfaces such as wood, fabric, plastic or paper. This is because the plasticizer (a chemical that keeps the clay soft) will leach, or seep out, leaving an oily residue that can damage or stain some surfaces. In some cases, plasticizer can actually be erosive.

You can also mold your clay pieces on glass panes with the edges ground or covered with stained-glass copper foil, which has an adhesive backing. This is especially helpful for pieces that will be baked flat, as it allows them to go from table to oven, remaining undisturbed until baked and cooled.

Conditioning

Before use, polymer clay must be kneaded into a workable form. This process is called conditioning. When you condition your clay, you are not only making it easier to handle, but you are actually moving the molecules closer together so that the clay will bake more efficiently.

Some types of clay, such as Fimo, are stiffer and require more conditioning. Others, like Sculpey III, are extremely soft right out of the package. It is important that you always condition your clay, even if it seems soft enough to use. Otherwise, it will be weaker and break more easily after baking. If unused clay becomes stiff, simply warm and knead it to make it workable again. For clay that is too soft, place it on a few pieces of paper and allow it to leach for a few hours or overnight to stiffen it.

The easiest way to condition clay is to knead small amounts at a time in your hands until it is pliable. Combine the smaller pieces of conditioned clay and continue kneading until the clay is soft and workable. Another way to condition clay is to crumble it into a plastic zipper bag and put it in your pocket. Your body heat will warm the clay and soften it.

Once polymer clay has been conditioned with your hands, it can be further conditioned by running it through a hand-cranked or motorized pasta machine. This also flattens conditioned clay into sheets in varying thicknesses.

Pasta machines have adjustable settings based on thickness. Although different brands may vary with the number of settings (some have seven, others have ten), #1 is the thickest setting on the pasta machine I used while making the projects in this book. If your machine is different, adjust the instructions accordingly. The steps below demonstrate the correct way to use the hand-cranked pasta machine to condition and flatten your clay.

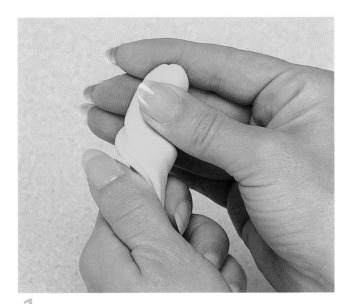

1 Begin by kneading a piece of clay in your hands to soften it. Once it is softened, flatten it into a sheet thin enough to be run through the pasta machine easily.

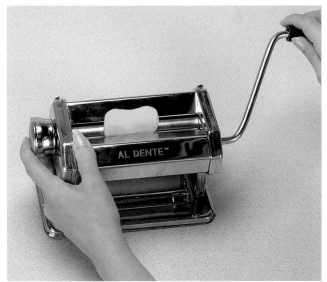

2 Run the clay through the pasta machine on setting #1, the thickest setting, then fold the clay in half and run it through the machine again on the same setting, fold-side first. *TIP: Always insert sheets into the pasta machine fold-side first to avoid air bubbles. The one exception is when making a Skinner blend circle cane, which is demonstrated on page 27.*

Baking

Polymer clay must be baked, or "cured," in order for it to harden completely. To avoid food contamination, I recommend baking your pieces in a toaster oven that you will only be using for clay. If you must use your home oven, be sure to take the proper safety precautions. (For safety information, see page 17.)

When baking your pieces, always follow the manufacturer's instructions. Generally, temperatures fall between 265°F–275°F (128°C–135°C) and times range from 20–30 minutes per ½" (1.3cm) thickness. Use an oven thermometer to check the accuracy of your oven, and always bake pairs together.

If possible, allow the clay to cool inside the oven, away from outside elements. If a piece is still warm when you remove it from the oven, allow it to cool completely on the baking surface before handling it. For added strength, re-bake the cooled piece for half the time.

When choosing a baking surface, keep in mind that different surfaces produce different results. Glazed ceramic tiles and glass panes with rounded or taped edges work best for baking completely flat pieces that don't require a soft finish on the back. Cardstock, typing paper and paper bags work best when baking two-sided pieces. Bead trays are best for baking round and tube beads, and they can be made with scrap clay, as shown on page 23. Lightbulbs are good for baking dome-shaped pieces, as in the Domed Daisy Pin on page 112.

Whatever surface you choose, make sure it is small enough to fit in the oven and able to withstand high temperatures.

Finishing

When polymer clay comes out of the oven, it has a slightly chalky appearance that is easily scratched. To give your polymer clay jewelry a satin finish, simply toss it in the washing machine. Place the jewelry in a lingerie bag and tie the bag tightly to secure. Place the bag in a second bag to keep the jewelry from escaping, and add a few strips of fabric from an old white shirt to keep the pieces from scuffing each other. Throw the bag in the washing machine and wash on a normal, bleach-free cycle. The result is a smooth, satin finish. If you prefer the shiny, glossy look for your jewelry, sand and polish it with wet/dry sandpaper, as described here.

Sanding and Polishing
Add a few drops of dish washing liquid to a bowl of water and sand the piece with 600-grit sandpaper while dunking repeatedly. Switch to 800-grit sandpaper, then 1000-grit, until you are satisfied with the appearance of your piece. The higher the grit, the smoother the piece will be. To finish, polish the piece with a soft cloth.

Following Safety Guidelines

Although polymer clay is labeled non-toxic, it is not to be used in conjunction with food items. Kitchen gadgets and tools can be of great use in polymer clay work, but they must be dedicated to the clay and never used in food preparation again. Your home oven can be used to bake the clay, but if you are going to do this frequently, a toaster oven is a worthwhile investment. If you are using your home oven, place your pieces in a large cake pan and cover it with another inverted cake pan as a lid. Never attempt to use a microwave oven to bake polymer clay.

If you smell burning plastic, turn off the oven immediately. Open the windows, run a fan and do not open the oven door. Not only is the smell unpleasant, but it is unhealthy to breathe the fumes of burning clay. Wait until the oven has cooled down completely and discard the burned piece. It is also a good idea to wipe down the sides of the oven interior with a paper towel. You can even reheat the empty oven to be sure the residue has dissipated before using the oven again.

It is also important to wash your hands after using polymer clay, particularly before preparing food or eating. You can use rubbing alcohol, soap and water or pumice, if needed, to remove any residue. Exam gloves are also an option. Not only do they keep your hands clay-free, but they also keep your pieces smooth and free from fingerprints.

Storing

Unbaked polymer clay can last for years if properly stored. Premo and Sculpey have an exceptionally long shelf life. Place opened packages of polymer clay in plastic zipper bags, then place these bags in plastic containers with lids. Always store unbaked polymer clay in a medium-to-cool environment. If clay is kept at extremely high temperatures, like in a hot car or on a window sill, it will actually start to bake.

Storing canes is a little more challenging. If the canes are touching each other, they will adhere to one another. Wrap individual canes with plastic food wrap before storing as above. For canes you will be using within days, you can lay them on tiles, glass or even sheets of paper. Keep in mind, however, that the paper will leach some of the plasticizer and stiffen the cane somewhat.

After your polymer clay jewelry has been baked, it should be treated as fine art. It should not be stored in areas that are subject to varied temperatures or in direct sunlight. This can fade the colors. If dropped, it likely will not break, but it is possible and it could get scratched. Polymer clay jewelry is not fragile, but it should be treated with care. Store each piece in a cloth bag or wrap it in soft fabric or tissue paper.

Mixing and Marbling

While it is true that polymer clay comes in a wide variety of colors, there may be a time when you want a marbled look or you can't find the exact color you need. In that case, you can always marble your clay or mix colors together to create your very own signature color.

1 Condition two pieces of clay (or as many as desired) in contrasting colors. Wrap one piece around the other and begin twisting.

2 For a marbled look, twist the clay until the desired look is achieved. For a completely blended look, continue twisting and kneading until there is no distinction between colors.

The techniques in this section are used in various projects throughout the book. As you will see, the steps are simple and the results are stunning. Refer back to these pages when a project calls for a blended or marbled sheet, an image transfer or beads made out of scrap clay. You can also use the color palette to transpose any of the projects in this book into one of ten beautiful color schemes.

Try These Mixing Recipes!

To make your clay:	*Add gradual amounts of:*
Lighter	White clay
Darker	Black clay
Toned down	Brown or gray clay
Lighter without changing hue	Translucent clay
Brighter	Fluorescent clay
Sparkle	Embossing powder or glitter
Pearly	Pearl clay
Metallic	Metal leaf or metallic clay
Speckled	Dried herbs and spices such as thyme, chili powder or ground black pepper
Flecked	Crayon shavings

Making a Skinner Blend

Developed by Judith Skinner, the Skinner blend is a method of shading clay by repeatedly rolling it through a pasta machine, resulting in beautiful and subtle color shifts.

1 Begin with two sheets of conditioned clay in contrasting colors, cut into squares. Cut each square in half and place one triangle of each color side by side to restore the square shape, as shown. Lightly smooth the seam where the triangles meet with your finger.

2 Fold the sheet so the colors match up. In this case, blue meets blue and white meets white.

3 Place the sheet fold-side first into the pasta machine and roll it through on the #3 setting.

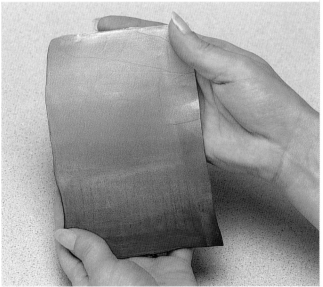

4 Repeat this process fifteen to twenty times or until the sheet is blended in a gradual shift from one color to the next.

Choosing a Color Palette

The projects and variations in this book reflect the ten color palettes shown below. The palette I used for each project is shown in the materials list, but not all of the colors listed for each palette are used every time the palette is used. For the ultimate creative experience, I challenge you to make the projects in palettes other than the ones I have used in my instructions. The combinations you choose are the elements that will make your projects one-of-a-kind.

Batik: blue, purple, red, green, translucent; all canes outlined in white

Blue: blue, black, white

Cloisonné: red, maroon, yellow, blue, purple, green, black; all canes outlined in gold

Earthy: white, ecru, chocolate brown, terra cotta, brown pearl (brown + pearl), mustard (yellow + brown + translucent), black

Jewel: blue pearl (blue + pearl), red pearl (red + pearl), green pearl (green + pearl), violet pearl (red pearl + blue pearl), gold, maroon, black

Neon: atomic orange, lemon yellow, lime green, hot pink, black

Noir: black, white

Opal: pearl, chocolate brown, silver, hot pink, olive pearl (orange + green + pearl), gold, lavender pearl (lavender + pearl), translucent pink (pink + translucent)

Salsa: red hot red, atomic orange, maroon, gold, copper, black

Tropical: blue, green, yellow, red, purple, orange, black

Transferring an Image onto Clay

Images can be transferred onto raw clay by means of a toner photocopy and acetone-based nail polish remover. Laser prints and copies will not work because they do not contain toner. It is the toner in the photocopy that transfers into the surface of the clay. Keep in mind that your transferred image will be a mirror of the original. This is especially important when transferring words.

1 Roll a sheet of conditioned light-colored clay through the pasta machine on the #5 setting. Be sure the surface is smooth and free of air bubbles. (You can pierce the bubbles with a needle.)

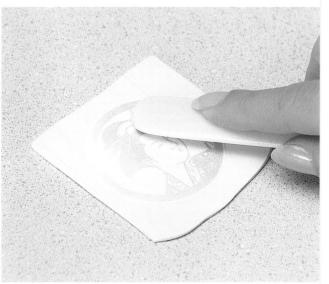

2 Using a cotton swab, coat the surface of the clay with nail polish remover. Lay the photocopy face-down on the wet clay. Burnish, or rub, the surface with a bone folder or the back of a spoon.

3 Keeping the photocopy on the clay, coat once again with nail polish remover. You will see the image through the back of the paper.

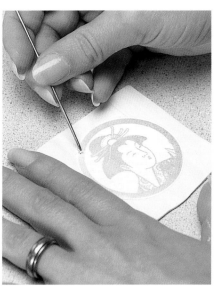

4 While the paper and clay are still damp, use a metal skewer to lift the paper from the clay.

5 Dip your finger in water and roll away any paper remnants to reveal the transferred image. Bake as directed. Once baked, the image is permanent.

Making Beads Out of Scrap Clay

Making beads is a great way to clean up your workspace and use scraps of clay at the end of a project. Beads can be strung onto necklaces and bracelets, made into earrings or used as embellishments for pins. Wearing snug-fitting exam gloves results in a smooth, fingerprint-free finish for the beads. Follow the instructions below to create round, tube, disc and slice beads.

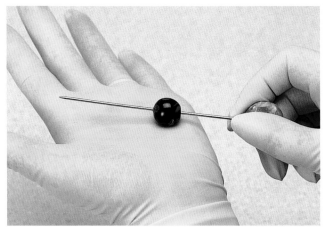

Round Bead

Roll a scrap of clay into a ball. Slowly pierce the ball with a metal skewer while turning the skewer until it pokes through the other side of the ball. Roll the skewered ball in your palm with light pressure to smooth it. Remove the round bead from the skewer, bake and cool.

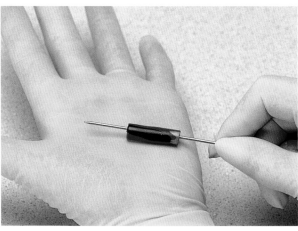

Tube Bead

Roll a ball of clay into a tube shape. Pierce the center of the tube with a skewer, then roll the tube on your work surface with your fingertips to achieve a smooth shape and finish. Remove the tube bead from the skewer, bake and cool.

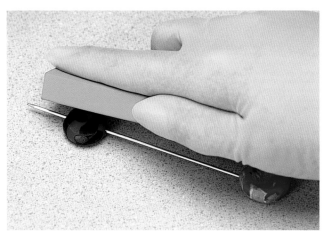

Vertical Disc Bead

For a disc bead with the hole running vertically, like a lollipop, roll a scrap of clay into a ball. Pierce the ball with a skewer, then lay the ball on your work surface and flatten it with an eraser.

Horizontal Disc Bead

For a disc bead with the hole in the center, like a doughnut, roll a scrap of clay into a ball shape, flatten it with an eraser, then pierce through the center with a skewer, as shown.

Slice Bead
Reduce a cane to the desired size. (You will learn how to make canes in the next section.) Use a tissue blade to slice beads from the cane. Pierce the beads with a metal skewer and flatten with an eraser.

Making Bead Trays Out of Scrap Clay

Unlike disc and slice beads, which are flat and can be baked on a ceramic tile, round and tube beads run the risk of developing flat, shiny spots when baked on a flat surface. Avoid this by baking them on bead trays made with scraps of clay and other tools, such as marbles and dowel rods, as shown below.

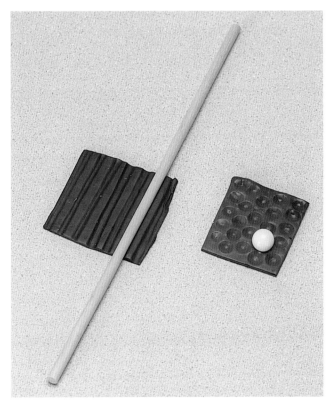

Bead Trays
Roll a sheet of scrap clay through the pasta machine on the #1 setting and place it on a ceramic tile. Press a marble or dowel into the clay to make indentations. Trim the sides with a tissue blade, bake and cool. Place raw clay beads into the indentations, bake and cool on the tray. *TIP: To keep the beads from sticking to the tray, dust the tray with baby powder every four or five bakings. The powder acts as a resist agent.*

CANES

Canes are rolls or stacks of polymer clay that are combined to make decorative shapes and patterns. They are usually made into long bars or logs and sliced to reveal a continuous design. An easy way to visualize canes is to think of holiday candy, where the design is embedded and repeated in each slice. Often, when people see the mixing of color and design in a polymer clay cane, they find it hard to believe that there is no painting involved.

Another word for caning is "millefiore," which means "a thousand flowers." It is illustrative of the glass paperweights made in Venice that display numerous flower canes encased in clear glass.

Pulling, pinching and rolling a cane, called reducing, will result in a longer, thinner log with the same cane pattern. Pushing the ends back together will enlarge the cane. Round canes can also be shaped into rectangles, triangles and other shapes by rolling the top, bottom and sides with an acrylic roller to flatten them. It is normal for cane ends to look like a mess of colored clay. It is when you slice into the cane that the pattern is revealed. Cane ends are great for rolling into beads. For easier slicing of canes, place them in the freezer for a few minutes.

In this section, you will find step-by-step instructions for fifteen canes, all of which look much more complex than they actually are. The colors used to build each cane are only for demonstration purposes and are not necessarily the colors used in the projects. The amount of clay needed and the diameter of a cane will also depend on the project and your own specific needs. As you begin to make the canes, you will be amazed at how easy it is to make an elaborate design in just a few simple steps.

Circle Cane

Use this simple cane as the basis for other caning techniques or to fill in your designs. Reduce or enlarge it to fit the size of your jewelry piece.

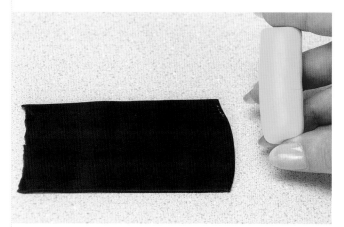

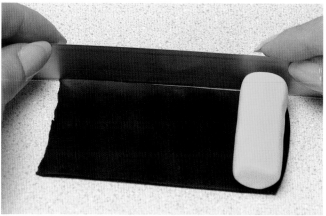

1 Roll a piece of conditioned clay through the pasta machine on the #4 setting and shape a contrasting piece of clay into a log.

2 Place the log onto the #4 sheet and use a tissue blade to trim away the excess clay from the top and bottom of the log.

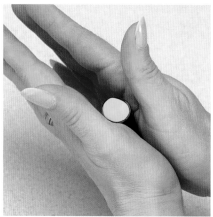

3 Roll the sheet all the way around the log to cover it completely. Trim the end with a tissue blade, angling the blade toward the log to make the seam easier to smooth.

4 Roll the log between your hands to smooth the seam.

5 Reduce as desired and slice to reveal the circle cane.

Skinner Blend Circle Cane

A variation on the circle cane, the Skinner blend circle cane is shaded from one color to another using the Skinner blend technique demonstrated on page 19.

1 Make a Skinner blended sheet as shown on page 19, then fold it into thirds with like colors touching. Roll the folded sheet through the pasta machine on the #1 setting to result in a long, thin strip of clay. This is the only time you will not insert the fold into the machine first.

2 Starting at either end, roll the entire strip into a short log. Roll a sheet of clay in a solid color through the pasta machine on the #4 setting. Wrap the sheet around the log and trim away the excess.

3 Roll the log between your hands to smooth the seam. Reduce as desired and slice to reveal the Skinner blend circle cane.

Ribbon Cane

The ribbon cane is just a flattened version of the Skinner blend circle cane. The subtle shading makes it a nice accent to floral designs.

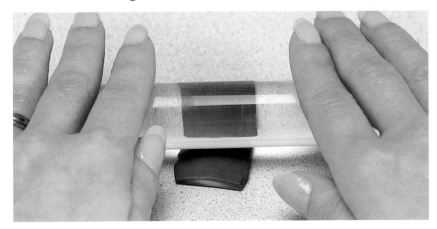

1 Make a Skinner blend circle cane as described above. Flatten the cane by pinching it with your fingers and rolling it with an acrylic roller.

2 Reduce as desired and slice to reveal the ribbon cane.

Stripe Cane

This cane, which is made by stacking sheets of clay on top of each other, makes a great stem for floral patterns. The thinner the sheets, the smaller the stripes will be. Try stacking several sheets in different colors and thicknesses to make an interesting design.

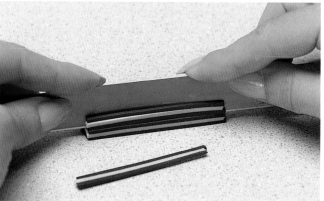

1 Roll two sheets of conditioned clay in contrasting colors through the pasta machine on the #6 setting. Cut the clay into rectangles and stack them, alternating the colors.

2 For a compound stripe, slice one stripe and, before removing it from the tissue blade, make a second slice. The two slices will stick together.

Spiral Cane

One of my favorite filler canes, the spiral cane is one of the easiest to make and is a classic design element. Make them in all different sizes and use them to create an interesting mosaic background for a pin or pendant.

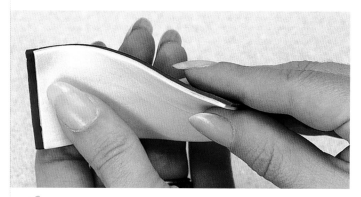

1 Roll two pieces of conditioned clay in contrasting colors through the pasta machine on the #5 setting. Trim them equally side to side, with one sheet ¼" (0.6cm) longer top to bottom. Center the smaller piece of clay on the larger one.

2 Pinch the clay together at one end and roll it into a spiral.

3 Reduce as desired and slice to reveal the spiral cane.

Flower Cane

A simple flower cane can be used alone or as a center for more elaborate flowers.
It begins with a large circle cane that is reduced and cut into equal pieces.

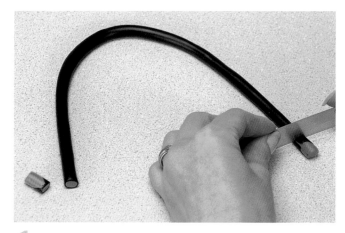

1 Make a circle cane as shown on page 26 and reduce it to a long, thin snake. Trim off the ends.

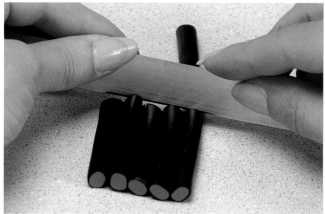

2 Cut the snake into six equal pieces. For accuracy, use the first piece to measure and cut the other pieces.

3 Make a second circle cane in a contrasting color and cut it to the same length as the pieces from step 2. Place the six cane pieces from step 2 around the new cane and press lightly to adhere.

4 Gently roll the cane between your palms to fuse all the pieces together. Be careful not to roll too hard or it will compress the flower.

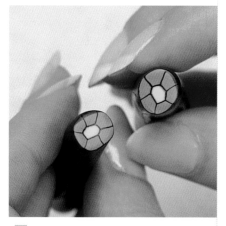

5 Reduce as desired and slice to reveal the flower cane.

Rose Cane

Surprisingly easy to make, the rose cane is made with flattened Skinner blend circle canes that are curved around a spiral center. Try making rose canes to represent different emotions: red for romantic love, pink or yellow for friendship and white for innocence.

1 Make a large Skinner blend circle cane as shown on page 27. Reduce the cane to graduated sizes and cut into several pieces.

2 Flatten each piece by pinching the edges with your fingers. Reduce as desired and cut each piece into three smaller pieces.

3 Roll one of the small pieces into a spiral shape. Place another small piece around the spiral.

4 Continue to place the flattened pieces around the spiral, overlapping the ends and getting larger as you go. Build up the rose cane with each additional section.

5 Press the cane together with your fingers and roll it on your work surface. Reduce as desired and slice to reveal the rose cane.

Simple Leaf Cane

By far the easiest leaf cane to make, this cane is both classic and contemporary.
It is made with a Skinner blend circle cane that is sliced and pinched into a leaf shape.

1 Make a Skinner blend circle cane as shown on page 27. Reduce as desired, then slice it into two pieces and place them side by side.

2 Press the canes together and pinch the top and bottom to give it a pointed leaf shape, as shown.

3 Reduce and shape as desired, then slice to reveal the simple leaf cane.

Veined Leaf Cane

This leaf cane takes a little more assembly, but the result is a very graphic and realistic leaf design. Vary your colors from vibrant yellow and neon green to forest green and chocolate brown, depending on the project's color palette.

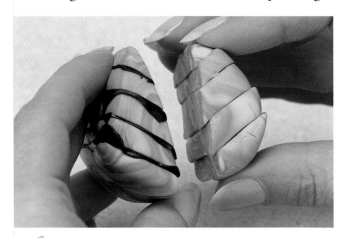

1 Make a marbled clay log as described on page 18. Pinch the log into a teardrop shape, then stand it up on one end. Cut the log in half, then cut each half into fifths. Roll a sheet of conditioned black clay through the pasta machine on the #3 setting. Place pieces of the #3 sheet in between the small sections and trim off the excess.

2 Roll another conditioned sheet of black clay through the pasta machine on the #2 setting. Sandwich the #2 sheet between the two large halves and trim away the excess.

3 Wrap the entire log with the remaining #3 black sheet from step 1 and trim away the excess.

4 Reduce the log as desired and slice to reveal the veined leaf cane.

Fan and Round Petal Canes

This cane can be pinched at one end to resemble a fan shape, or pinched at both ends to resemble a round shape. Either way, the result is a beautiful petal that can be used alone or in layers to create your favorite flowers.

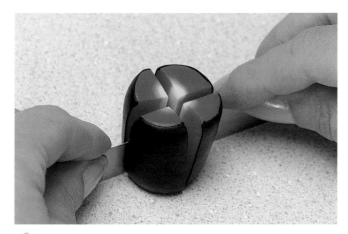

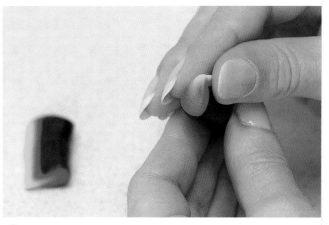

1 Make a Skinner blend circle cane as shown on page 27. Stand the cane on end and slice it into fourths. Set two of the pieces aside for use in another project.

2 Pinch the two remaining pieces into teardrop shapes and reduce equally as desired.

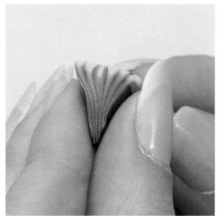

3 Place the pieces side by side and press them together to form one bar.

4 Cut the bar in half and place the halves side by side. Repeat this process. You should now have a cane with eight sections. To make a fan petal cane, pinch one side of the bar, tapering it all the way down the length of the cane. Reduce as desired and slice to reveal the cane.

5 To make a round petal cane, pinch the top and bottom into a petal shape. Reduce as desired and slice to reveal the cane.

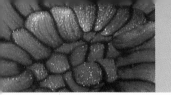

Leaf Petal Cane

Made just like a fan petal cane in leaf colors, this design can look tropical and almost painted. Slice larger leaves from the cane to decorate larger pieces such as pendants, then reduce the cane and slice tiny leaves for matching earrings.

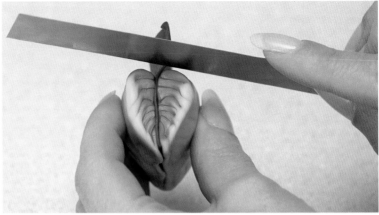

1 Follow steps 1-4 from the fan petal cane on page 33, using the colors you desire for your leaf. Pinch each section into a teardrop shape, tapering the edges with the lighter-colored clay. Reduce as desired.

2 Roll a sheet of conditioned clay in a contrasting color through the pasta machine on the #2 setting. Insert the #2 sheet between the halves and trim off the excess.

3 Press the halves together and reduce, making sure to pinch the top of the leaf to keep it pointed.

4 Reduce as desired and slice to reveal the cane.

Simple Star Cane

This easy cane is perfect for making beads or as an accent. With the right color combination, it makes a great retro design.

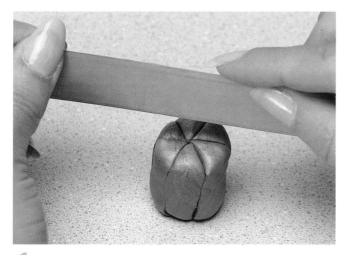

1 Roll a piece of clay into a short log, stand it on end and slice it into six sections.

2 Roll a sheet of conditioned clay in a contrasting color through the pasta machine on the #3 setting. Cut it into strips slightly longer than the log and sandwich the strips between the sections. Press the sections back together.

3 Reduce as desired and slice to reveal the star cane.

Multi-Layered Cane

Although you won't see this cane in any of the projects in this book, you can use it to dress up any cane by incorporating these fun and easy ideas. You'll be amazed at how fancy a simple cane can become with just a few extra layers of clay.

1 Roll sheets of conditioned clay through the pasta machine on various settings. Wrap the sheets around the cane and trim off the excess.

2 Roll out skinny snakes of clay in contrasting colors and wrap them around the cane. Press gently into the cane with your fingers and roll between your palms. Reduce as desired.

3 Add more layers around the cane, continuing as desired to make several layers. Reduce as desired and slice to reveal the multi-layered cane.

Crackle Cane

The translucent clay in this cane allows you to see right through it, and the thin lines of contrasting color give it a crackled appearance. The crackle cane acts as a great overlay for gold leaf, as in the Crackle Pin on page 76. Don't be concerned about keeping the cane bars too square while reducing. This will give you a more natural crackled appearance.

1 Roll a block of translucent clay into a log. Roll a sheet of conditioned clay in a contrasting color through the pasta machine on the #1 setting and wrap it around the log. Trim off the excess.

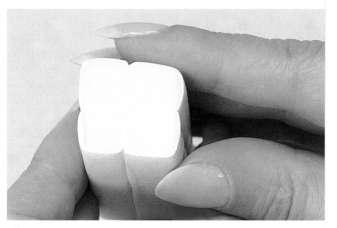

2 Reduce the log and cut it into four pieces. Flatten each piece into a square and stack them together to make a square bar, as shown.

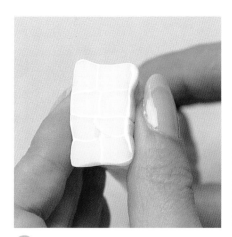

3 Trim the ends, reduce the cane again and cut in half. Place the halves side by side to form a rectangular bar.

4 Cut the bar in half again and re-stack to make sixteen sections. The bar will be square again.

5 Continue to stack and reduce in this manner until a crackle design appears. Slice to reveal the crackle cane.

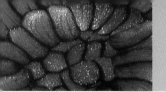

Mokume Gane Cane

The term "mokume gane" (pronounced mo-KOO-may GAH-nay) means wood grain. This technique was originally used in Japanese metalsmithing. Different objects and shaped clay cutters will produce various effects, and no two sheets are exactly alike.

1 Roll three sheets of conditioned clay in contrasting colors through the pasta machine on the #5 setting. Stack the sheets on top of each other and roll them through on the #5 setting again.

2 Cut the sheet of clay in half and stack one half on top of the other. Continue cutting and stacking in this manner as desired.

3 Press a paintbrush handle into the top of the layered clay block to make indentations. Press small and large clay cutters randomly into the top of the block.

4 Bend the tissue blade into an arc and make curved cuts randomly into the top of the block. Do not cut all the way through the block.

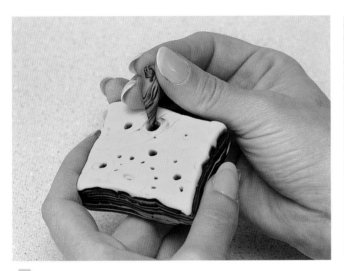

5 Roll scraps of clay into small, elongated cones. Place the cones into the holes made in step 3.

6 Compress the block by pushing it in on the sides and top. Reduce as desired.

7 Use your tissue blade to make extremely thin slices, revealing the mokume gane cane.

8 Roll a sheet of conditioned dark-colored clay through the pasta machine on the #1 setting. Cover the #1 sheet with the thin slices. Smooth the surface with an acrylic roller or roll the entire sheet through the pasta machine to result in a beautifully blended mokume gane design sheet, as shown.

PROJECTS

Now that you know how to construct beautiful canes, it is time to use them! You will notice that some canes are used repeatedly in the projects. For instance, the fan petal cane can be used as flower petals or butterfly wings. The simple leaf cane can be used alone or repeated on a stem to become a vine. These projects are designed to be used as they are presented in the following pages and also as a springboard for creating your own variations.

If you are looking for new ways to use polymer clay, or you have always wanted to try it but didn't know where to start, these projects are for you. I have designed them to be user-friendly as well as beautiful. My designs come by way of experimentation, interpretation and repetition. I enjoy the challenge of something new. I just jump in and I don't care if I make a mistake. The most important thing to know is that mistakes are a wonderful learning tool. In fact, most mistakes lead to new ideas!

Several of the projects require templates or transfer images, which I have provided on pages 124–125. Photocopy them all at once and cut them out as you need them. Or, you can also trace the templates onto stencil plastic with permanent marker and cut them out to use again and again.

Twenty projects, twenty-two variations and ten color palettes give you a world of possibilities to try. Using the basic design of a project, you can change the shape, style, size, and in the case of the image transfer projects, the art. This is your book, so get creative and have fun!

Leaf Face Pin

This pin would make a great gift for a gardener or anyone who loves plants. Using small slices of leaf and flower canes, this project is much easier than it looks. I used a flexible face mold by Polyform to make the face. Molds like this are available in many different shapes, sizes and styles. An exercise in repetition, this framed face is a friendly accent pin that offers a whimsical touch of the natural world.

Palette

Tropical

Clay

⅛ block white ● ⅛ block black ● Veined leaf cane (page 32): lemon yellow and lime green with #2 black veins, wrapped in #2 black and reduced to ¾" (1.9cm), ½" (1.3cm) and ¼" (0.6cm) ● Flower cane (page 29): lemon yellow and atomic orange circle canes wrapped in #2 black, reduced to ¼" (0.6cm) and ⅛" (0.3cm) ● Circle cane (page 26): hot pink wrapped in #1 black, reduced to pinhead size

Tools and Materials

Flexible face mold (Polyform) ● Water ● Pinback ● Tissue blade ● Craft knife ● Jewelry adhesive (E6000)

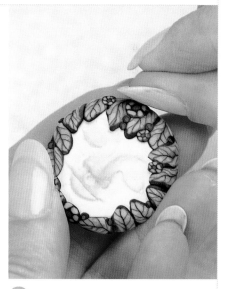

1 Roll a marble-sized piece of white clay into a ball. Rub water on the surface of the clay and press it into the mold. Flex the mold to release the clay. Bake and cool. Press the face into a marble-sized ball of black clay.

2 Position thin leaf cane slices around the face and smooth them with your fingernail.

3 Add flower and circle cane slices to fill in the design. Bake and cool. Score the back of the pin with a craft knife and adhere a pinback with jewelry adhesive. To further secure the pinback, cover the attached bracket with a pinch of black clay, bake and cool.

Link Bracelet

This sturdy yet delicate bracelet is fun to make, wear or give as a gift. The one demonstrated here is made with polymer clay slice beads cut from a rose cane, but you can use round, tube and disc beads, as well. Once you have mastered making bead links from purchased eye-pins, these bracelets take little time to complete. Add more links for an anklet or less for a child's wrist.

Palette

Opal

Clay

Rose cane (page 30): hot pink and white Skinner blend circle cane wrapped in #4 hot pink

Tools and Materials

Eyepins • Headpin • Jump ring • Clasp • Rosary pliers • Needle-nose pliers • Tissue blade • Metal skewer

1 Make several slice beads from the rose cane. (For instructions, see page 22.) Bake and cool. Slide a bead down an eyepin until it meets the loop.

2 Snip the remaining wire from the eyepin to ¼" (0.6cm).

3 Loop the remaining end of the eyepin so that it rests snug against the bead.

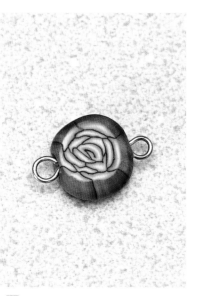

4 With the pliers still in the loop, rock the loop in the opposite direction, then back again. This will give you a nice, round loop.

5 The bead should look like the one pictured above. Repeat steps 2–4 with the desired number of beads for your bracelet.

6 To connect the bracelet, hold one loop of one of the beads between your thumb and forefinger and open the other loop by twisting it sideways with the pliers.

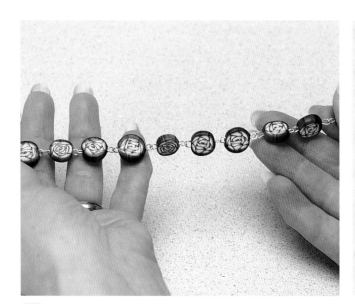

7 Slip the closed loop of the next link onto the open loop, then re-close the loop by twisting it back in the other direction. Continue this process with the remaining beads.

8 Use pliers to add one end of the clasp to the last link on one end of the bracelet. Repeat with the other end of the clasp and bracelet.

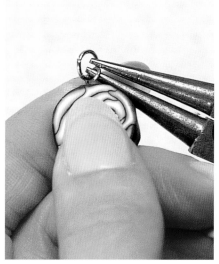

9 To make a dangle that hangs from the bracelet or the clasp, slip a bead onto a headpin and slide it down to the head. Snip the other end of the headpin to ¼" (0.6cm) and make a loop as in steps 3 and 4.

10 Open a jump ring by grasping it between rosary and needle-nose pliers and twisting the pliers in opposite directions at the seam. Use rosary pliers to attach the jump ring to the loop on the bead dangle.

11 Attach the jump ring of the dangle to the bracelet at the end of the clasp. Close the jump ring by twisting it the other way with the pliers.

Earthy Bead Bracelet

This bracelet features round beads made of scrap clay and slice beads from a spiral cane. The varied sizes and shapes give the piece an eclectic charm.

Palette

Jewel

Goddess Pendant

Your personal goddess begins as an orb—of course!
Her face is framed with delicate canes, and her body is
hand-molded into a form easily achieved and infused
with your special touch. As the clay is manipulated, the
metal leaf breaks into tiny fragments and the cane slices
distort and swirl. The original quality of this pendant is
further enhanced by using matching beads made from
scrap clay.

Palette

Jewel

Clay

⅛ block black • ⅛ block white • Scraps of clay and scrap clay beads (page 22) • Mokume gane cane (page 38): gold, red pearl, blue pearl and green pearl, sliced and rolled into a #2 sheet • Crackle cane (page 37): translucent and copper, reduced to 1" (2.5cm) • Star cane (page 35): gold and black wrapped in #2 black, reduced to ¼" (0.6cm) and ⅛" (0.3cm) • Circle cane (page 26): gold wrapped in #1 black, reduced to ⅛" (0.3cm) and pinhead size

Tools and Materials

Flexible face mold (Polyform) • Water • Soft cloth • Metal leaf • Water-based oil paint in burnt sienna • Metallic E beads • Necklace chain • Two eyepins • Headpins • Rosary pliers • Tissue blade • Craft knife • Paintbrush with plastic handle • Exam gloves (optional)

1 Roll a ball of scrap clay to about 1" (2.5cm) in diameter. Cover the ball with the mokume gane sheet and smooth the seams with your fingers.

2 Add pieces of metal leaf and slices of crackle cane to the ball.

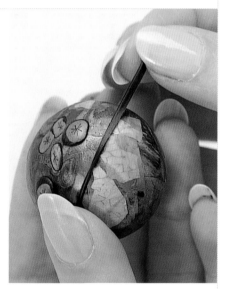

3 Add thin snakes of black clay around the ball. Roll the ball between your palms to smooth the surface.

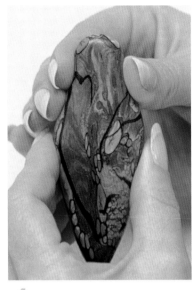

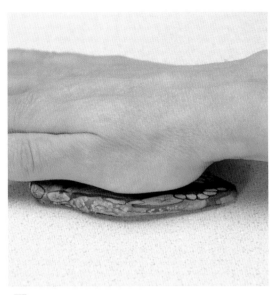

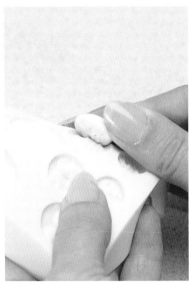

4 Mold the clay ball into the desired goddess body shape with your fingers.

5 Gently press the goddess body flat, turn it over and flatten again.

6 Roll a marble-sized ball of white clay. Wet the surface of the face mold with water, then push the clay ball into the mold. Flex the mold to release the clay, bake and cool.

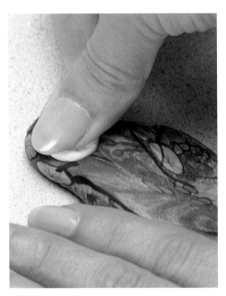

7 Press the baked white face into the top of the goddess body.

8 Frame the face and neck areas with star and circle cane slices.

9 Insert the loops, or eyes, of the eyepins into the goddess body on each shoulder. Pinch the clay to secure. Bake and cool. Trim the eye-pins to ¼" (0.6cm) and shape them into loops with the rosary pliers.

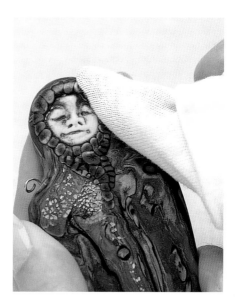

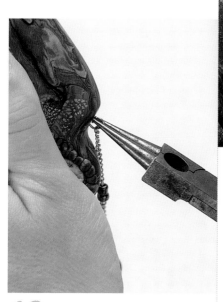

10 Antique the face by painting it with water-based oil paint, then wipe it clean with a soft cloth.

11 Cut a necklace chain into several 1" (2.5cm) pieces and reconnect them with E beads and scrap clay beads in between. (For instructions, see steps 2–7 from the Link Bracelet project on pages 45–46.)

12 Attach the ends of the chain to the eyepins on the goddess body. Close with pliers.

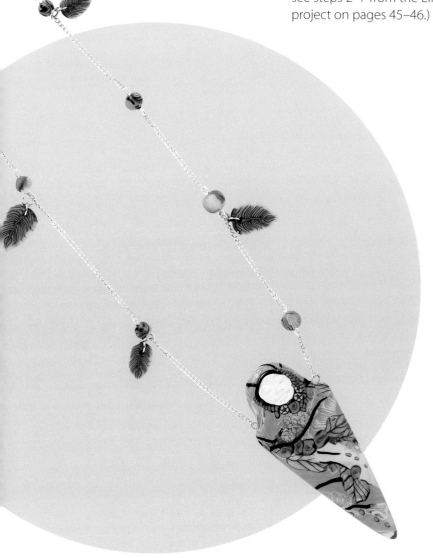

Mother Nature Pendant

Thinner and more angular, this goddess illustrates the variations that occur from hand-molding. I added leaf canes around her face and leaf slice beads as dangling accents.

Palette

Neon

Butterfly Pin

Cloisonné is an enameling technique where pieces of colored glass are built up in between thin channels of metal. This playful pin uses a classic butterfly motif to mimic the cloisonné technique. It is important that all canes be wrapped in gold clay to represent the metal channels. The Skinner blended background is the perfect complement to the faux cloisonné design. The simple black border frames this shimmering pin.

Palette

Cloisonné

Clay

⅛ block black ● Red and maroon Skinner blended sheet (page 19) ● Fan petal cane (page 33): blue pearl and gold Skinner blend circle cane with #1 black veins, wrapped in #3 gold and reduced to ½" (1.3cm) ● Simple leaf cane (page 31): green pearl and gold Skinner blend circle cane wrapped in #3 gold, reduced to ½" (1.3cm) ● Spiral cane (page 28): #7 black and #1 gold, reduced to ½" (1.3cm) ● Circle canes (page 26): purple, red and black, each wrapped in #3 gold, reduced to pinhead size

Tools and Materials

Wet/dry sandpaper ● Water ● Soft cloth ● Pinback ● Acrylic roller ● Tissue blade ● Scissors ● Craft knife ● Jewelry adhesive (E6000) ● Cardstock ● Butterfly Pin template (page 124) ● Pasta machine

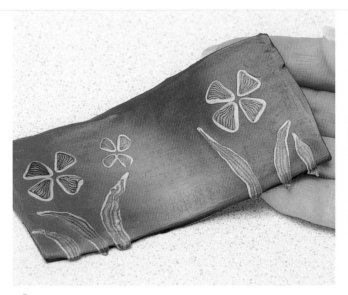

1 Run the Skinner blended sheet through the pasta machine on the #5 setting. Trim it to 4" x 2½" (10.2cm x 6.4cm). Construct a butterfly design on the sheet using fan petal cane slices as butterfly wings and simple leaf cane slices as grass. Flatten with an acrylic roller.

2 Add spiral and circle cane slices to fill in the design, then smooth the surface with an acrylic roller.

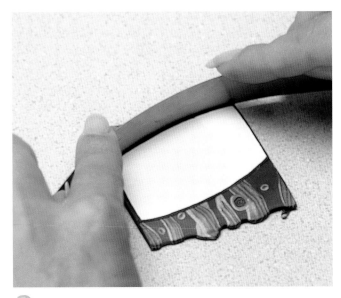

3 Copy and cut out the template, place it over the design and cut out the shape with the tissue blade.

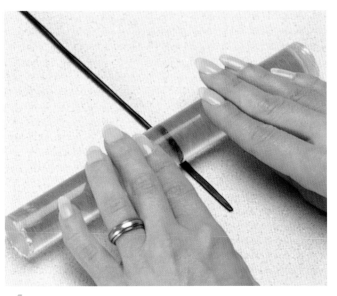

4 Roll a long, thin snake out of black clay and flatten it with the roller.

5 Apply the flattened snake to the top edge of the pin. Lightly press it into place and trim, leaving a little excess at the edges. Apply another snake to the bottom of the pin, press into place and trim.

6 Add black borders to the sides of the pin in this manner, as well.

7 Smooth the corners with your fingernail.

8 Use the tissue blade to apply light pressure against the outside of the clay to adhere the borders. Bake and cool.

9 Sand and polish the baked piece. (For instructions, see page 16.) Score the back with a craft knife and adhere a pinback with jewelry adhesive. To further secure the pinback, cover the attached bracket with a pinch of black clay, bake and cool.

Mini Butterfly Pin

Cut from the same design sheet, this miniature version is cut into a different shape and has no border. To make smaller butterflies, reduce the canes further before slicing.

Palette

Cloisonné

Shield Pendant

The best thing about polymer clay is that there is no waste. Even the scraps are ripe with design potential. End pieces from canes make especially interesting patterns. When scrap pieces are rolled into a ball and then flattened, the result is a colorful, abstract design that is different every time. Subtle shadings and swirls are beautifully unplanned and unique. Make the beads in this project from the same scraps to give the pendant a custom look.

Palettes

Salsa and Neon

Clay

½ block black ● Assorted canes in Salsa and Neon palettes ● Stripe cane (page 28): #3 red and #3 black ● Scrap clay beads, one with a large hole (page 22)

Tools and Materials

Super stretchy elastic cord ● Black, red, green and yellow E beads ● Two large jump rings ● Rosary pliers ● Needle-nose pliers ● Acrylic roller ● ⅜" (1cm) circle cutter ● Tissue blade ● Scissors ● Pasta machine ● Superglue ● Cardstock ● Shield Pendant template (page 124)

1 To make side one, run a sheet of conditioned black clay through the pasta machine on the #7 setting. Trim the sheet to about 4" x 5" (10.2cm x 12.7cm) and set the remainder of the sheet aside for use in step 3. Add slices of assorted canes in rows so that they touch each other. Flatten and fuse the pieces together with an acrylic roller.

2 Cut a slice of the stripe cane and leave it on the tissue blade. Cut another stripe directly below it to make a compound stripe. Lay the stripes between the rows of canes and flatten with the roller. Set this piece aside for use in step 6.

3 To make side two, roll half of the remaining black clay from step 1 into a ball. (You will use the rest of the black clay in step 6.) Place a few assorted cane slices over the ball and roll it smooth with your hands.

4 Flatten the ball with your fingers and run it through the pasta machine on the #5 setting.

5 Place more assorted cane slices over the #5 sheet and roll with an acrylic roller.

6 Retrieve side one and place it cane-side down on your work surface. Place the remaining #7 black sheet from step 3 over it, then layer side two over the #7 black sheet, cane-side up. This process is called "sandwiching."

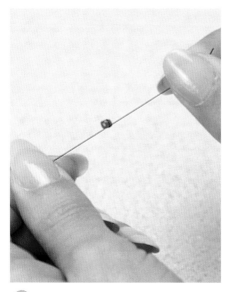

7 Copy and cut out the shield template and place it over the layered design sheet. Use a bowed tissue blade to cut out the shield shape through all layers.

8 Use a ⅜" (1cm) circle cutter to punch a hole in the top center of the shield. Bake and cool. *TIP: If you dip the cutter in water beforehand, it will release easier. The water works as a release agent for the clay.*

9 To assemble the necklace, cut a piece of cord to the desired length for your necklace and securely knot an E bead at one end. This is called a stopper bead, and it keeps the other beads from sliding off the cord. It will be removed in step 11.

 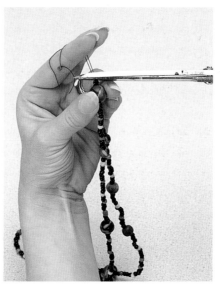 

10 Hold the cord in one hand and string several E beads onto the cord with the other hand. Add a scrap clay bead, then more E beads. Continue until you have reached the desired length for your necklace. Finally, thread the scrap bead with the large hole onto the cord.

11 Knot the cord three or four times at the base of the last bead to create a compound knot. Trim the cord ends close to the knot, including the end with the stopper bead from step 9. Add a dab of superglue to the compound knot and slip it through the large hole in the bead to secure and hide it.

12 Open one of the jump rings as described on page 47, steps 10 and 11. Slip it through the hole in the pendant and around the necklace cord, then twist the other way to close it. Add a second jump ring through the hole in the pendant in the same manner.

Light the Night Pendant

This pendant uses glow-in-the-dark clay, so it glows under a black light! You can create scrap pendants in many different shapes, sizes and color palettes, and you can even make mini-shield earrings to match!

Palette

Neon

Mermaid Pin

I used one of my original watercolor paintings for this project. Unlike the transfer technique, which leaves a toner imprint of the image in the clay, this technique requires making a color print-out or copy of an image, cutting it out and actually embedding it into the clay. A layer of Translucent Liquid Sculpey (TLS) protects and seals the image, making it a permanent part of the pin. Cane slices are layered on the background like a mosaic. Once you have made this pin, try making a pin with your own artwork, photos or quotes.

Palette

Blue

Clay

½ block black ● Assorted canes in Blue palette ● Translucent Liquid Sculpey (TLS)

Tools and Materials

Pinback ● Acrylic roller ● Tissue blade ● Scissors ● Craft knife ● Paintbrush with plastic handle ●
Toothpick ● Pasta machine ● Glue (Aleene's Reverse Collage Glue) ● Jewelry adhesive (E6000) ●
Cardstock ● Mermaid image (page 125)

1 Make a color copy of the mermaid image onto cardstock. Cut out the image along the blue border.

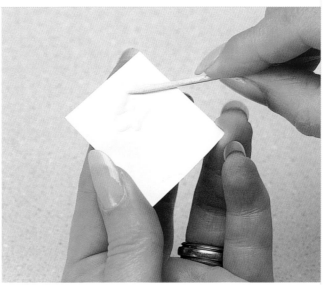

2 Spread an even amount of glue on the back of the image with a toothpick. (I recommend using Aleene's Reverse Collage Glue because it adheres to plastic.) Make sure to spread the glue to the edges.

3 Run a sheet of conditioned black clay through the pasta machine on the #5 setting. Cut the sheet in half and set one half aside for use in step 5. Place the mermaid image on the remaining #5 black sheet and use a tissue blade to trim the clay to about ⅛" (0.3cm) around the border of the image. Use a paintbrush to coat the image and border with TLS. Bake and cool.

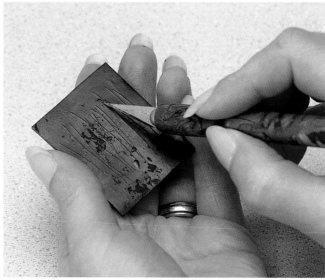

4 Once the mermaid piece is cool, score the back with a craft knife. Place the piece aside for use in step 7. The score marks will help the piece grab the adhesive.

5 Trim the remaining #5 black sheet from step 3 to about 3" x 2½" (7.6cm x 6.4cm). Slice assorted canes to about 1/16" (2mm) and arrange them side by side on the sheet, covering it almost all the way to the edges.

6 Gently roll the slices with an acrylic roller to fuse them, but do not flatten them. The surface should have some dimension and resemble a mosaic.

7 Apply a small amount of TLS to the back of the baked piece from step 4 and place it in the center of the mosaic piece. Press down firmly to adhere.

8 Trim the sides of the mosaic piece, leaving a ¼" (0.6cm) border on each side of the image.

9 Round the corners with your fingernail, then bake and cool. To finish, score the back of the baked piece with your craft knife and adhere a pinback with jewelry adhesive. To further secure the pinback, cover the attached bracket with a pinch of black clay, bake and cool.

Sun Goddess Pin

The image used in this piece is very different from the mermaid image. The bold colors and graphic lines are complemented by the simple black and white. Try it or any of the other transfer images on page 125 with this technique.

Palette

Noir

Floral Tile Bracelet

Tiled blocks and colorful E beads are the elements that make up this floral bracelet. It makes a statement as a colorful accessory, but becomes a real conversation piece when flipped to show the reverse. The tropical design makes it perfect for a cruise, pool party or anytime you need a splash of color and fun. A six-tiled bracelet fits me, but you will need to measure your own wrist to assess how many tiles you will need to make for a comfortable fit.

Palette

Tropical

Clay

1½ blocks black ● ½ block blue + ½ block green, marbled (page 18) ● Flower cane (page 29): yellow and red circle canes wrapped in #1 black, reduced to ¼" (0.6cm) and ⅛" (0.3cm) ● Fan petal cane (page 33): red and yellow Skinner blend circle cane wrapped in #1 black, reduced to ½" (1.3cm) ● Veined leaf cane (page 32): blue and green Skinner blend circle cane with #1 blue veins, wrapped in #4 blue and reduced to ½" (1.3cm) ● Mokume gane cane (page 38): red, yellow, blue, green and black ● Spiral cane (page 28): red and yellow Skinner blend circle cane, flattened and rolled into a spiral with #1 black sheet, reduced to ½" (1.3cm)

Tools and Materials

Thin elastic cord ● Red and black E beads ● Acrylic roller ● Rectangular clay cutter ● Scissors ● Tissue blade ● Metal skewer ● Rubber eraser ● Pasta machine

1 To make side one, run the blue and green marbled sheet through the pasta machine on the #6 setting, then trim it to 10" x 2½" (25.4cm x 6.4cm). Arrange thin slices of flower canes randomly on the marbled sheet to form flower centers. Then, arrange thin slices of the fan petal cane around the flower centers to form petals.

2 Add thin slices of the veined leaf cane to complete the pattern. Flatten the cane slices with an acrylic roller.

3 Lift the sheet from your work surface by sliding the tissue blade underneath with one hand and lifting the sheet carefully with your other. Set it aside for use in step 6.

4 To make side two, run a sheet of conditioned black clay through the pasta machine on the #6 setting. Trim it to 10" x 2½" (25.4cm x 6.4cm) and set the leftover black clay aside for use in step 6. Decorate the remaining #6 sheet with mokume gane cane slices and flatten with an acrylic roller.

5 Apply spiral cane slices randomly onto the sheet, then roll flat again with the roller.

6 Run the remaining black sheet from step 4 through the pasta machine on the #7 setting. Sandwich the #7 black sheet between side one and side two, making sure the canes are facing out on both sides. Smooth and flatten the stack with the roller.

7 Lightly impress the rectangular cutter into the surface of the clay to make impressions. Do not cut through the clay, as this will be done with the tissue blade in step 8.

8 Cut straight down through all the layers of the clay with the tissue blade along the impressions to create tiles. The number of tiles you make will depend on the desired length of your bracelet.

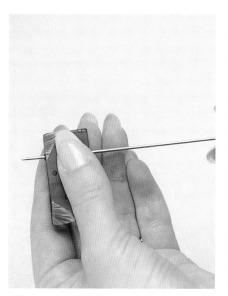 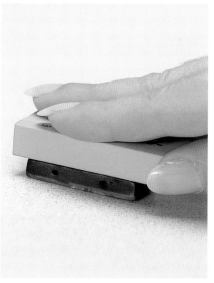 

9 Using the metal skewer, drill two equally-spaced holes through the black center layer of each tile. Use a turning motion as the skewer travels through the clay. Remove the skewer.

10 Using the blank side of a rubber eraser, gently press down on the surface of the tiles to flatten them. Bake and cool.

11 To finish the piece, string the elastic cord through the holes in each tile, inserting two red E beads and two black E beads in between each tile. Knot the cord several times and trim the ends. Place a dab of superglue onto the knots and pull them through a tile hole to conceal.

Glimmering Bracelet

This is an elegant version of the bracelet that features all tiles and no beads. Light travels up and down the flower petals as it reflects on the mica particles in the metallic clay.

Palette

Jewel

Tiled Pin

This project features a dimensional framing technique made up of cane slices. The result is an intricate tile pattern with a decorative marquee design at the top and bottom. Make a color copy of the photo provided on page 125, or scan your own photo and print it out on a color printer. Consider using vintage photos of parents or grandparents, baby pictures and even photos of pets.

Palette

Jewel

Clay

1 block black • Flower cane (page 29): gold and copper circle canes wrapped in #1 black, reduced to ³⁄₁₆" (0.5cm) and ¹⁄₈" (0.3cm) • Simple leaf cane (page 31): copper wrapped in #1 black, reduced to ³⁄₈" (1cm) • Simple leaf cane (page 31): green pearl wrapped in #1 gold, reduced to ³⁄₈" (1cm) • Fan petal cane (page 33): copper, gold and maroon wrapped in #1 copper, reduced to ¹⁄₂" (1.3cm) and ¹⁄₄" (0.6cm) • Translucent Liquid Sculpey (TLS)

Tools and Materials

Pinback • Tissue blade • Scissors • Craft knife • Toothpick • Pasta machine • Glue (Aleene's Reverse Collage Glue) • Jewelry adhesive (E6000) • Cardstock • Photo image (page 125)

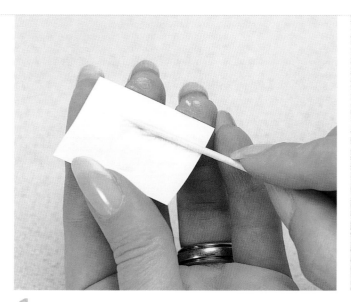

1 Color copy and cut out the antique photo and use a toothpick to coat the back with glue. (I recommend Aleene's Reverse Collage Glue.)

2 Run a sheets of conditioned black clay through the pasta machine on the #5 setting. Cut the sheet in half and set one half aside for use in step 5. Adhere the photo to the remaining black sheet and smooth the surface with your fingernail.

3 Trim a 1/16" (2mm) clay border around the photo with the tissue blade and coat the entire surface with TLS. Bake and cool, making sure the piece is completely cool so the photo stays flat.

4 Score the back of the baked piece with your craft knife.

5 Trim the remaining #5 black sheet from step 2 to 1¾" x 2" (4.5cm x 5.1cm). Apply TLS to the back of the baked piece and press it into the center of the raw piece.

6 Arrange flower, simple leaf and fan petal cane slices around the photo to frame it.

7 Add more cane slices in a second layer, above and below the photo.

8 Add more cane slices as desired. Bake and cool. Score the back of the pin with a craft knife and adhere the pinback with jewelry adhesive. To further secure the pinback, cover the attached bracket with a pinch of black clay, bake and cool.

Big Top Pin

Miniature cane slices can be arranged in numerous ways for one-of-a-kind frames. Notice how the star cane adds a bit of the circus to this jester pin.

Lady of the Sea Pin

Here is another example of the mermaid image, cropped closer than in the mosaic pin and used as a black and white transfer image, then decorated with colored pencils.

Palette

Jewel

Palette

Salsa

Fidget Pendant

Inspired by pop art, this necklace features movable parts that give your hands something to do when you feel fidgety. It is a simple but sculptural design with geometric components made up of stark, contrasting cane patterns. The center bead, which seems to float in the middle of the pendant, is made from a slice from a spiral cane. To learn more about making and baking slice beads, see page 19.

Palette

Noir

Clay

1 block black • 1 block white • Stripe cane (page 28): #3 black and #3 white • Spiral cane (page 28): # 3 black and #3 white, reduced to ½" (1.3cm) and ⅜" (1cm) • Skinner blend circle cane (page 27): black and white wrapped in #1 black, reduced to ¼" (0.3cm) and pinhead size

Tools and Materials

Rubber cord • One black E bead • Wet/dry sandpaper • Soft cloth • Two headpins • Rosary pliers • Acrylic roller • Tissue blade • ⅜" (1cm) circle cutter • Pasta machine

1 Run one sheet each of black and white clay through the pasta machine on the #5 setting. Cut two 1¾" x 2¼" (4.5cm x 5.7cm) pieces out of the white sheet and three 1¾" x 2¼" (4.5cm x 5.7cm) pieces out of the black sheet. Make a striped stack as shown, reserving one black piece for the next step. Set the striped stack aside for use in step 5.

2 To make side one, place the remaining black piece from step 1 on your work surface. Cut thin slices from a stripe cane and lay them side by side on a slant across black piece.

3 Layer spiral cane slices on top of the stripes and flatten with an acrylic roller.

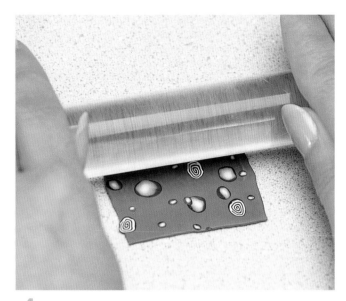

4 To make side two, mix the remaining black and white clay until it is completely blended into gray, then run it through the pasta machine on the #3 setting. Decorate the gray sheet with spiral and Skinner blend circle canes, then roll flat.

5 Trim the striped stack from step 1 to 1½" x 2½" (2.5cm x 3.8cm) and set one of the trimmed scraps aside for use in step 8. Sandwich the stack between side one and side two, making sure both decorative sides are facing outward.

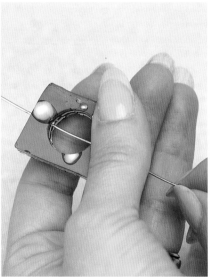

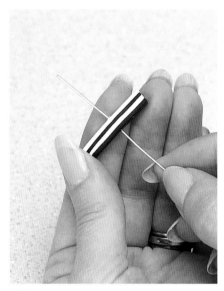

6 Wet the circle cutter and press it into the center of the decorated block. Remove the cutout and trim the sides of the block to 1" x 1½" (2.5cm x 3.8cm). Round the corners with your fingernail.

7 Carefully pierce through the bottom of the block, through the hole and up through the top of the block with a headpin.

8 Make a slice bead from a spiral cane. (For instructions, see page 23.) Trim the scrap from step 5 to a 1¼" x 3/16" (3.2cm x 0.5cm) bar and pierce both the bead and the bar through the center with the remaining headpin. Bake and cool all pieces with headpins still in place. Sand and polish as desired.

9 Remove the headpins and place the slice bead inside the hole in the decorated block. Holding the bead in place, reinsert a headpin through the bottom of the block, through the bead and out the top of the block.

10 Add a black E-bead and the striped bar to the headpin.

11 Trim the headpin to ⅜" (1cm) and bend it into a loop with pliers. Trim the rubber cord to the desired length for your pendant, string it through the loop, knot the ends and trim.

Fidget Earrings

Using headpins, assemble the earrings as shown. Trim the headpins, bend into loops and hang from earring findings. Try making the pendant and earrings in bright or pastel colors to match your favorite outfit.

Palette

Noir

Crackle Pin

In this pin, metal leaf is layered beneath the surface of translucent crackle cane slices to give it dimension. Metal leaf comes in between pieces of tissue paper and is very delicate. However, embedded beneath polymer clay, it will be forever preserved. This pin uses variegated leaf, which features blue and green swirls that complement the blue palette.

Palette

Blue

Clay

½ block blue • ½ block black • Crackle cane (page 37): white and translucent, reduced to 1" (2.5cm) • Large spiral cane (page 28): #3 white and #3 blue wrapped in #1 blue, reduced to ½" (1.3cm) • Small spiral cane (page 28): #3 white and #3 blue wrapped in #1 black, reduced to ⅛" (0.3cm)

Tools and Materials

Pinback • Metal leaf • Acrylic roller • Tissue blade • Scissors • Craft knife • Pasta machine • Jewelry Adhesive (E6000) • Cardstock • Crackle Pin template (page 124)

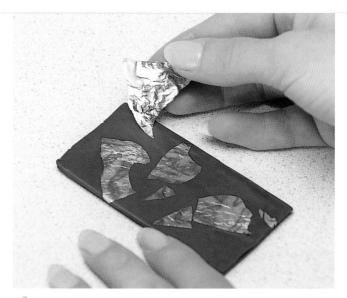

1 Run a sheet of conditioned blue clay through the pasta machine on the #4 setting, then run a sheet of conditioned black clay through on the #1 setting, reserving a small pinch of black clay to be used for the border. Layer the #4 blue sheet on top of the #1 black sheet. Pick up pieces of metal leaf with your index finger and arrange them randomly onto the blue sheet. The metal leaf will stick immediately and cannot be removed.

2 Cover the entire blue sheet with thin slices from the crackle cane.

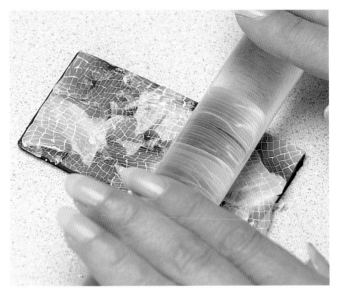

3 Flatten with an acrylic roller.

4 Arrange thin slices of the large and small spiral canes randomly on top of the crackle cane slices. Flatten again with the roller.

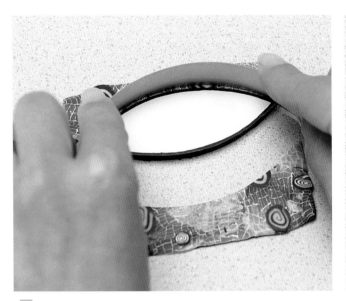

5 Copy and cut out the template, place it over the sheet and use a tissue blade to cut out the shape.

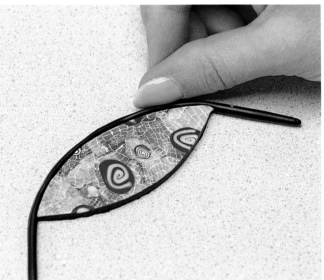

6 Roll a long, thin snake out of black clay and press it with your fingernail to flatten it against one side of the pin. Trim at the points.

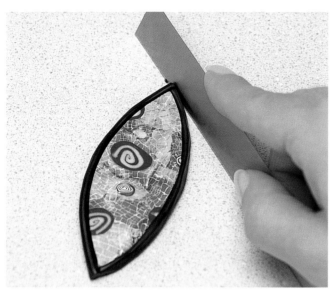 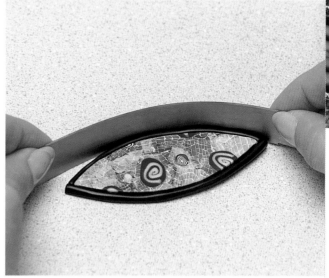

7 Repeat on the other side and trim off the excess.

8 Press the edge of the tissue blade against the border to flatten it, as shown. Bake and cool. Score the back of the baked piece with a craft knife, then attach a pinback with jewelry adhesive. To further secure the pinback, cover the attached bracket with a pinch of black clay, bake and cool.

Woodgrain Pin

This version of the crackle pin has the appearance of wood. I used gold leaf instead of variegated leaf, which complements the warm hues of the earthy palette.

Palette

Earthy

Tribal Choker

This choker with a tribal charm uses a technique that looks very much like batik, a fabric-dyeing technique in which the parts of the fabric not intended to be dyed are covered with removable wax. The metal choker wire finishes the piece with minimal assembly. Black clay is impressed with the same pattern as the colored clay, but because the colored area is rolled smooth after impressing, the design is much larger and looser. The contrast between the impression and the dye-like pattern of the colored area is striking.

Palette

Salsa

Clay

2 blocks black, divided into five pieces ● ½ block orange, divided into two pieces ● ¼ block copper ● ¼ block red hot red ● Assorted scrap clay beads with large holes (page 22)

Tools and Materials

Spirals texture sheet (Polyform) ● Wire choker with twist-off bead end ● Water ● Acrylic roller ● Craft knife ● Tissue blade ● Bamboo skewer ● Pasta machine ● Cardstock

1 Run sheets of copper, atomic orange and red hot red clay through the pasta machine on the #1 setting. Stack the orange sheet on top of the copper sheet, then add torn pieces of the red sheet over the orange sheet. Run the stack through the pasta machine on the #2 setting.

2 Run one conditioned black sheet through the pasta machine, one on the #2 setting and another through on the #1 setting. Sandwich the layered sheet from step 1 between the two black sheets, with the #2 black sheet on top.

3 Wet the surface of the stack with water and place the texture sheet on top of it. Impress the texture by rolling firmly with an acrylic roller. Remove the texture sheet and use a craft knife to scratch random lines into the surface of the stack.

4 Holding the tissue blade flat against the stack, begin shaving the surface. The colored clay will begin to show through. Set this sheet aside for use in step 6.

5 Run a sheet of orange through the pasta machine on the #3 setting, then run a sheet of black through on the #4 setting. Layer the orange sheet on top of the black sheet and apply the clay shavings from step 4, colored-side up.

6 Run each design sheet through the pasta machine on the #5, #6 and #7 settings to flatten. Run another sheet of conditioned black clay through the pasta machine on the #5 setting and imprint the texture as described in step 3.

7 Trim the black textured sheet and colored design sheet to two strips each, measuring ½" x 2¼" (1.3cm x 5.7cm). Trim the remaining black sheet to 1" x 3¼" (2.5cm x 8.3cm) and the remaining colored sheet to 1" x 2¼" (2.5cm x 5.7cm). Arrange on your work surface as shown above. Side one of the pendant is on the left and side two is on the right.

8 Run another sheet of conditioned black clay through the pasta machine on the #5 setting. Layer side one over it and lightly roll with an acrylic roller, making sure not to flatten the texture.

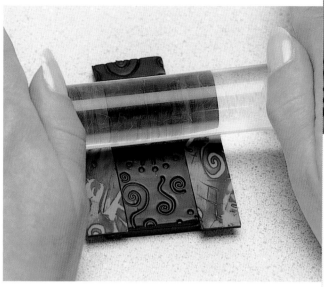

9 Trim side one to 1½" x 2¼" (3.8cm x 5.7cm).

10 Flip side one over and layer side two on top of it. Lightly roll with the roller.

11 Flip the pendant back over and trim the bottom and the sides of the top, leaving the flap at the top center intact.

12 Lay a bamboo skewer at the top of the flap and roll toward the pendant. Lightly press the roll against the top of the pendant to adhere it. Bake and cool on card-stock with the skewer in place.

13 Twist off the end from the wire choker. Remove the skewer from the pendant and string the choker with the pendant in the center and scrap clay beads on both sides. Twist the end back on to the choker.

Bamboo Pin

Inspired by the Japanese lacquer items of the 1950s, this pin uses iridescent "snowflake" confetti, which is like glitter, to mimic mother-of-pearl fragments that were often inlayed as a light-catching accent. The flakes will shrink during baking and sanding, so don't be afraid to use large pieces. The canes are cut thickly because when they are rolled flat, the black outline distorts, resulting in an effect that looks like hand-painted shading.

Palette

Jewel

Clay

½ block black ● ⅛ block gold ● ¼ block green pearl + ¼ block blue pearl, marbled (page 18) ● Large circle cane (page 26): gold wrapped in #2 black, reduced to ½" (1.3cm) ● Small circle cane (page 26): red pearl wrapped in #1 black, reduced to pinhead size ● Simple leaf cane (page 31): gold wrapped in #1 black, reduced to ¼" (0.6cm) ● Spiral cane (page 28): #3 blue pearl and #3 black, reduced to ¼" (0.6cm)

Tools and Materials

Iridescent snowflake confetti ● Metal skewer ● Jewelry adhesive (E6000) ● Pinback ● Acrylic roller ● Craft knife ● Scissors ● Tissue blade ● Pasta machine ● Cardstock ● Bamboo Pin template (page 124)

1 Run a sheet of conditioned black clay through the pasta machine on the #2 setting, reserving a small pinch to make a border in step 9. Run the marbled clay through on the #3 setting. Layer the marbled sheet on top of the black sheet. Use a metal skewer to sketch three lines into the surface of the clay. This will mark the placement of the bamboo stalks.

2 Cut a ⅛" (0.3cm) slice from the large circle cane, pinch it in the center and flatten the ends with your fingernail. The slice should resemble a bone, as shown in the slice on the right. Repeat to make several more.

3   Place the slices end-to-end along the lines you made in step 1 to form the bamboo stalks. Press down to fuse them together.

4   Add thin slices of the simple leaf, spiral and small circle canes and roll the sheet smooth with an acrylic roller.

5   Copy and cut out the template and place it over the sheet. Trace the shape onto the raw clay with the back of your craft knife.

6   Sprinkle a few flat pieces of confetti inside the outline and press down to embed them into the surface of the clay.

7   Cut out the shape with a tissue blade.

8 Roll a snake of gold clay about ⅛" (0.3cm) thick and cut it in half. Place one half against the top straight edge of the pin and the other half against the bottom. Trim the gold borders flush with the sides.

9 Repeat step 8 with a black snake and the curved sides of the pin. Trim flush with the gold borders at the top and bottom.

10 Add one more gold snake at the top of the pin and one at the bottom, trimming them flush with the black border. Use your tissue blade to even out all the sides. Bake and cool. Score the back of the piece with a craft knife and adhere a pinback with jewelry adhesive. To further secure the pinback, cover the attached bracket with a pinch of black clay, bake and cool.

Subtle Elegance Pin

The earthy palette renders this pin a study in color value and texture. The soft browns have a subtle elegance against the silky pearl background.

Palette

Earthy

Wearable Vessel

Sure to be a favorite accessory, this vessel is an inspirational and wearable work of art. Fill it with special messages, trinkets or clay poetry stones made with word transfers. The eyelets in the lid are a nice finishing touch. What a great gift for yourself or a friend—a handmade vessel filled with a special surprise.

Palette

Earthy

Clay

1 block black • ½ block white + ½ block ecru, marbled (page 18) • Simple leaf cane (page 31): ecru and terra cotta Skinner blend circle cane wrapped in #1 chocolate brown, half reduced to ¼" (0.6cm) to make leaves, half rolled to #6 sheet to make vines • Stripe cane (page 28): #3 black and #3 ecru, stacked and trimmed to 6" (15.2cm) • Flower cane (page 29): ecru and terra cotta Skinner blend circle canes wrapped in #1 chocolate brown, reduced to ¼" (0.6cm) and ⅛" (0.3cm) • Spiral cane (page 28): #3 ecru and #3 chocolate brown, reduced to ¼" (0.6cm) • Circle cane (page 26): brown pearl wrapped in #1 black, reduced to pinhead size

Tools and Materials

Paper towels and core from roll • Cardstock • Aluminum foil • Plain white paper • Nylon cord • Two eyelets • Embossing powder in chocolate brown • Acrylic roller • Tissue blade • Scissors • Craft knife • Paintbrush with plastic handle • Metal skewer • Pasta machine • Double-sided tape • Superglue

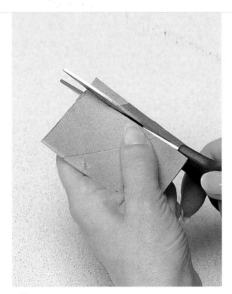

1 To make the vessel, flatten a paper towel core and trim it to 3" (7.6cm) long. Cut it open and lay flat on your work surface. Reserve the rest of the core for use in step 10.

2 Fold one end in ¼" (0.6cm) to make a flap. Apply double-sided tape to the flap and close the core again to form an ellipse shape. Trim the excess if necessary.

3 Fill the ellipse with a few paper towels to hold the shape, then wrap it in aluminum foil.

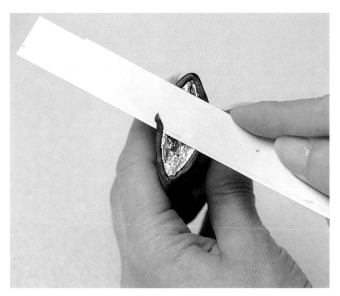

4 Run a sheet of conditioned black clay through the pasta machine on the #6 setting. Wrap the sheet around the ellipse and use your tissue blade to trim the clay flush with the top and bottom. Set the excess #6 sheet aside for use in step 6.

5 Smooth the seam with your fingernail.

6 Place the ellipse on top of the remaining #6 sheet of black clay from step 4. Roll the tube on the surface of the sheet to adhere it.

7 Using a tissue blade, cut the excess clay from around the tube to create the bottom of the vessel. Repeat this process to make the top of the vessel.

8 Use the paintbrush handle to poke two holes in the top of the vessel, ½" (1.3cm) in from each side. Then, make one hole in the bottom center of the vessel.

9 Use a metal skewer to make an indentation all the way around the vessel, ¾" (1.9cm) down from the top. This will mark the position of your lid.

10 Make a clean, continuous cut in the indentation with your tissue blade, but do not separate the upper and lower halves. Cut open the remaining paper towel roll, flatten it and insert a sheet of plain white paper to make a cradle for the vessel. Bake and cool the vessel in the cradle to help retain its shape.

11 Re-insert the tissue blade into the cut you made in step 10 and carefully separate the upper and lower halves. Pull both pieces off the foil form.

12 Insert your craft knife into the holes you made in step 8 and turn it a few times to widen and clean the holes.

13 Run the marbled clay through the pasta machine on the #4 setting. Apply thin slices of the simple leaf and stripe canes to create leaves and vines. Fill in the design with flower, spiral and circle canes as desired, then sprinkle embossing powder on the surface to add decorative flecks of color. Flatten the design sheet with an acrylic roller.

14 Combine the leftover scraps of black clay and run through the pasta machine on the #5 setting. Layer the design sheet from step 13 on top of the #5 black sheet and trim to 1¾" x 4" (4.5cm x 10.2cm). Set the excess clay aside for use in step 17. Wrap the remaining clay sheet around the lower half of the vessel and smooth the seam with your fingernail. Follow steps 6 and 7 to make another bottom for the vessel.

15 Use the paintbrush handle to poke through the raw clay into the hole in the bottom of the vessel. Bake upright on a piece of cardstock and allow to cool.

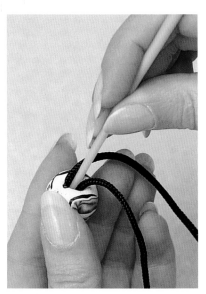

16 Cover the remaining black area on the vessel (the lip) with a strip of foil. Smooth the foil and tuck the excess inside the vessel. Re-insert the foil form from step 11 into the vessel and replace the lid.

17 Trim the remaining design sheet from step 14 to 1¼" x 4" (3.2cm x 10.2cm) and wrap it around the lid of the vessel. Smooth the seam and make another black clay top as you did in steps 6 and 7. Poke through the holes with the paintbrush handle. Slice a continuous piece of the stripe cane and apply it around the bottom of the lid. Bake and cool.

18 Roll a large round bead from a scrap of your remaining clay. Cut a long piece of nylon cord, fold it in half and press the folded end into the bead with the paintbrush handle.

19 Use a pinch of clay to cover the cord and fuse it by rolling the paintbrush handle over the clay. Make another round bead the same size, then make a horizontal disc bead out of black clay. (For instructions, see page 22.) Make sure the holes in the beads are large enough to accommodate both ends of the cord. Bake and cool.

20 Remove the foil and use your craft knife to enlarge the holes at the top and bottom of the vessel to the size of your eyelets. Add a dab of superglue to each hole and insert the eyelets.

21 Apply superglue to the ends of the cord to stiffen them, then thread the vessel as follows: round scrap bead (fused to cord in steps 18 and 19), black disc bead, vessel bottom, vessel lid, round scrap bead. Knot the cord, trim the ends and add more superglue if desired. The round bead on top helps to hold the vessel closed and can slide up and down the cords.

Poetry Stones

Poetry stones are the perfect surprise to hide inside the wearable vessel. To make them, type the words of your choice in your favorite fonts. You will want to make the words small—about ½" (1.3cm) maximum—so that they will fit inside the vessel. Print out mirror images of the words and transfer them onto small pinches of light-colored clay, as described on page 27.

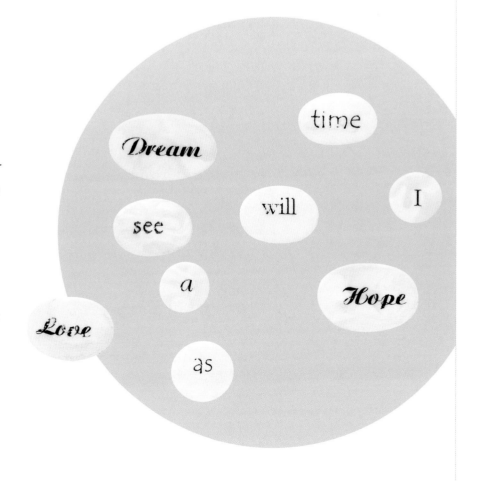

Chrysanthemum Fan Pin

The detailed chrysanthemum design of this pin looks far more complicated than it is. Made up of repetitive rings of round petal cane slices, the chrysanthemum seems to blossom with each step. The petals beautifully display the subtlety of the Skinner blend, and the pearl clay lends a satin sheen to this classic floral pin. For a flower with less petals, like a daisy, simply use larger cane slices and fewer layers.

Palette

Opal

Clay

½ block black ● ¼ block pearl and ¼ block gold, marbled (page 18) ● Round petal cane (page 33): hot pink and pearl Skinner blend with #1 chocolate brown veins, wrapped in #1 chocolate brown and reduced to ⅜" (1cm), ¼" (0.6cm) and ³⁄₁₆" (0.5cm) ● Circle cane (page 26): lavender pearl wrapped in #1 chocolate brown, reduced to pinhead size ● Veined leaf cane (page 32): olive pearl with #1 chocolate brown veins, wrapped in #1 chocolate brown and reduced to ⅜" (1cm) ● Ribbon cane (page 27): pearl and chocolate brown Skinner blend circle cane wrapped in #1 chocolate brown, reduced to 1¼" (3.2cm)

Tools and Materials

Pinback ● Acrylic roller ● Tissue blade ● Scissors ● Craft knife ● 1" (2.5cm) circle cutter ● Pasta machine ● Jewelry adhesive (E6000) ● Cardstock ● Chrysanthemum Fan Pin template (page 124)

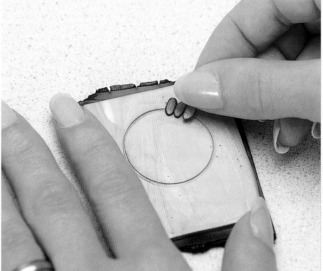

1 Run the pearl and gold marbled clay through the pasta machine on the #5 setting, then run a sheet of black through on the same setting. Trim the marbled sheet to 2¾" x 2" (7cm x 5.1cm) and layer it over the black sheet. Lightly press the circle cutter into the surface of the sheet to make an impression, but do not press hard enough to cut through the clay.

2 Slice several petals from the ⅜" (1cm) round petal cane and arrange the canes in a single layer around the impressed circle.

3 Repeat with the ¼" (0.6cm) round petal cane, arranging the slices inside the first circle.

4 Repeat with the ³⁄₁₆" (0.5cm) round petal cane, arranging the slices inside the second circle. Flatten the entire sheet of clay with an acrylic roller.

5 Place several thin slices from the circle cane in the center of the flower and press with your finger to adhere.

6 Add veined leaf and ribbon cane slices around the flower to form leaves and a stem, then add more circle cane slices to the background to fill in the design. Smooth with the roller.

7 Copy and cut out the template. Place it on the design sheet and cut out the fan shape with the tissue blade. Round the corners with your fingernail, then bake and cool.

8 Score the back of the pin with a craft knife and adhere a pinback with jewelry adhesive. To further secure the pinback, cover the attached bracket with a pinch of black clay, bake and cool.

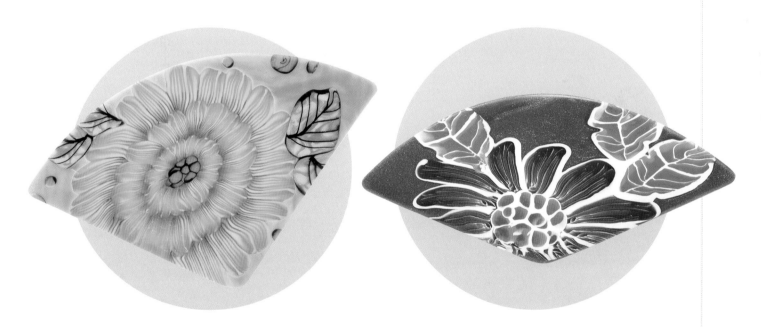

Island Flower Pin

In the neon palette, the chrysanthemum fan pin has more of an island feel, bright and graphic.

Simple Daisy Pin

This pin uses one ring of large petals to make a simpler daisy. Notice the slightly different shape, which was cut by hand.

Palette

Neon

Palette

Batik

Asian Pendant

This pendant features image transfers using reproductions of my original ink drawings that I tinted with colored pencils and antiqued with water-based oil paint. Unlike acrylic paint, which lays on top of clay, water-based oil paint seeps into the surface, giving it a deep, waxy look that is soft, warm and organic. You will never have to worry about this pendant flipping to the back side because it is just as interesting on the reverse. It makes a lovely wall hanging when not being worn.

Palette

Salsa

Clay

½ block black, divided in half ● ⅛ block white + ⅛ block ecru, blended (page 18) ● Red and maroon Skinner blended sheet (page 19) ● Assorted canes in Salsa palette ● Horizontal disc bead and tube bead made from scrap clay (page 22) ● Translucent Liquid Sculpey (TLS)

Tools and Materials

Rubber cord ● Embossing powder in copper ● Water-based oil paint in burnt sienna ● Gold wax ● Colored pencils ● Nail polish remover ● Cotton swab ● Bone folder or spoon ● Water ● Soft cloth ● Acrylic roller ● Tissue blade ● Scissors ● Craft knife ● 2" (5.1cm) circle cutter ● Metal skewer ● Two paintbrushes with plastic handles ● Pasta machine ● Superglue ● Cardstock ● Geisha and crane transfer images (page 125) ● Exam gloves (optional)

1 Transfer the geisha and crane images onto the light ecru clay as described on page 21. Center the circle cutter over each image and press down to cut them out. Set the images aside for use in step 5.

2 Run both pieces of black clay through the pasta machine on the #7 setting. Set one sheet aside for use in step 3 and cover the remaining sheet with thin slices from assorted canes. Roll the sheet with an acrylic roller to fuse the slices. This becomes side one.

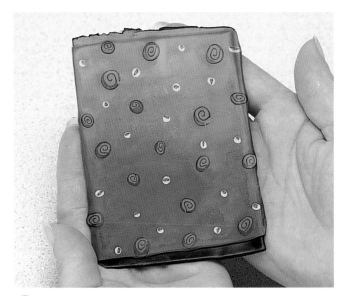

3 Layer the red and maroon Skinner blended sheet on top of the remaining #7 black sheet and arrange thin cane slices on top of it sparsely, as shown. Roll the sheet with an acrylic roller to flatten it. This becomes side two.

4 Place the Skinner blended sheet cane-side down, then place the patterned sheet from step 2 over it, cane-side up. The #7 black sheets will be sandwiched in between the two decorated sheets.

5 Place the geisha transfer image on one side of the patterned clay and gently pat it down with your fingers to adhere it. Use a tissue blade to trim the sheet to 3¼" x 3¼" (8.3cm x 8.3cm).

6 Flip the pendant over and repeat step 5 with the crane image. Round the corners with your fingernail.

7 Roll two small beads of black clay with your fingers. Place the beads on the top of the pendant and flatten them with your fingernail, making clay grommets.

8 Using a metal skewer, drill channels into the clay grommets, about ¾" (1.9cm) deep. Make sure the channels are wide enough to accommodate the cord. Bake and cool on cardstock.

9 Color in the details of the transfer images with colored pencils, leaving some areas white for contrast.

10 Apply a coat of TLS onto the geisha image with a paintbrush.

11 Lightly sprinkle a small amount of copper embossing powder onto the image, avoiding the face area. This antiquing technique is called "flyspecking." Bake and cool, then repeat on the other side.

12 Use your craft knife to score tiny lines into the surface of your pendant on both sides. Brush the pendant with burnt sienna water-based oil paint, scrubbing it into the lines. Coat the entire surface on both sides. *TIP: To avoid getting paint on your hands, I recommend wearing exam gloves.*

13 Wipe away the majority of the paint with a soft cloth. Rub the center of the image more vigorously so that the edges are darker and the image is clear. Allow the paint to dry.

14 Dip a soft cloth into gold wax and lightly rub it onto the grommets, the edges of the pendant and the images to give them a metallic sparkle. Allow the wax to set for at least a day, or bake the piece in the oven for five minutes. *TIP: It is important that you allow oil paint and wax plenty of time to dry so that they do not rub off on clothing or skin.*

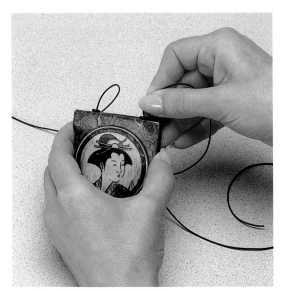

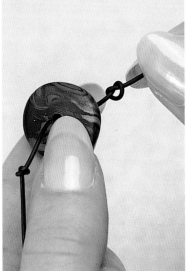

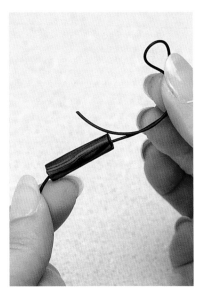

15 To make the necklace cord, cut two 12" (30.5cm) lengths of rubber cord and apply drops of superglue to one end of each cord. Insert the superglued ends into the channels of the grommets.

16 Tie a knot about 3" (7.6cm) from the end of one of the cords. String a horizontal disc bead onto the cord and make another knot to secure the bead. Trim the end of the cord to the knot.

17 String a tube bead onto the other cord and loop the end of the cord, as shown.

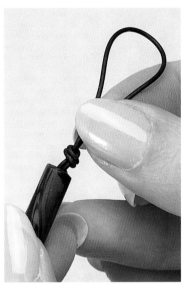  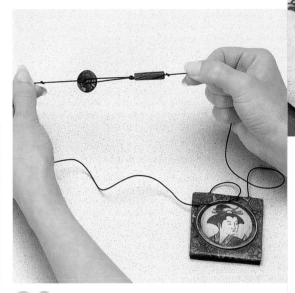

18 Knot the loop, making sure it is big enough to fit over the disc bead. Trim the end of the cord and secure the knot with a dab of superglue. Slide the tube bead up the cord and tuck the knot into the hole in the bead to conceal it.

19 Tie another knot at the bottom of the tube bead.

20 Slip the disc bead into the loop to make a toggle clasp.

Asian Pendant

The Cloud Serpent, shown here, decorates one side of this pendant, and the Mayan Moon Goddess decorates the other side. Both images can be found on page 125. They are accented by the metallic colors of the jewel palette.

Palette

Jewel

Egyptian
Princess Pin

A texture sheet provides an interesting raised surface on the background of this pin. My Egyptian Princess drawing is transferred onto light-colored clay, then antiqued with water-based oil paint and gold wax. This gives the piece an air of mystery.

Palette

Earthy

Clay

⅛ block black ● ⅛ block ecru ● Translucent Liquid Sculpey (TLS)

Tools and Materials

Texture sheet (Polyform) ● Pinback ● Nail polish remover ● Cotton swab ● Bone folder or spoon ● Water in a spray bottle ● Soft cloth ● Water-based oil paint in burnt sienna ● Gold wax ● Acrylic roller ● Tissue blade ● Craft knife ● Two paintbrushes with plastic handles ● Pasta machine ● Jewelry adhesive (E6000) ● Cardstock ● Large Egyptian Princess transfer image (page 125) ● Exam gloves (optional)

1 Run a piece of conditioned black clay through the pasta machine on the #7 setting. Spritz the sheet with water. The water acts as a release agent so the texture sheet won't stick to the clay in the next step.

2 Place the texture sheet over the clay.

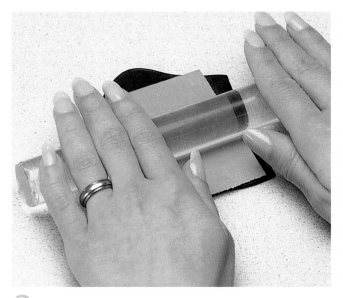 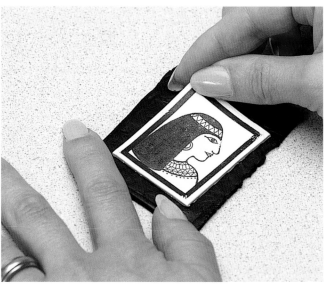

3 Using an acrylic roller, slowly and firmly roll over the texture sheet to make an impression in the clay. Remove the texture sheet and make sure you have a good impression. If you don't get the desired texture, flatten the clay and try again.

4 Run a piece of conditioned ecru clay through the pasta machine on the #5 setting and transfer the Egyptian Princess image onto the clay as described on page 21. Use a tissue blade to trim around the image just outside the black border. Place the clay with the transferred image on the textured black sheet and trim the black sheet to about $1/4$" (0.6cm) from the image.

5 Round the corners of the piece with your fingernail.

6 Use a paintbrush to spread TLS over the image. Bake and cool.

7 Score the surface of the baked piece with a craft knife, then brush water-based oil paint onto the piece and wipe it off with a soft cloth. Leave the edges darker than the center. Allow the paint to dry.

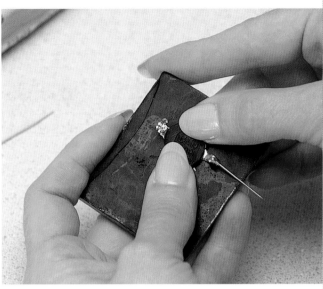

8 Apply gold wax highlights to the piece. Allow the wax to set for at least a day, or bake in the oven for about five minutes.

9 Score the back of the piece with a craft knife, then adhere a pinback with jewelry adhesive. To further secure the pinback, cover the attached bracket with a pinch of black clay, bake and cool.

Mayan Moon Goddess Pin

Using the Mayan Moon Goddess art completely changes the flavor of this pin. It uses a deeper texture sheet, which makes the gold wax highlights more prominent.

Cleopatra Pin

This pin uses gold clay and a finer texture for the background. I also tore the edges of the top layer of clay and highlighted the piece with gold embossing powder.

Palette
Earthy

Palette
Earthy

Egyptian Princess Earrings

For this project, the Egyptian Princess motif is reduced and reversed so that you will have mirror image earrings. These earrings are lovely as an ensemble to the Egyptian Princess Pin on page 104. They are comfortable to wear, surprisingly lightweight for their size and have nice movement, thanks to French hook earring wires. This demonstration shows how to make one earring, but I recommend making both at the same time.

Palette

Earthy

Clay

½ block black • ¼ block white + ¼ block ecru, marbled (page 18) • Translucent Liquid Sculpey (TLS)

Tools and Materials

Two headpins • Two French hook earring wires • Nail polish remover • Cotton swab • Bone folder or spoon • Soft cloth • Colored pencils • Water-based oil paint in burnt sienna • Gold wax • Rosary pliers • Rubber eraser • Tissue blade • Two paintbrushes with plastic handles • Pasta machine • Cardstock • Small Egyptian Princess transfer image (page 125)

1 Run the marbled clay through the pasta machine on the #5 setting. Transfer the small Egyptian Princess image onto the marbled clay as described on page 21. Trim just outside the border with a tissue blade. Run a sheet of black clay through on the #7 setting and layer the Egyptian Princess image on top of the sheet.

2 Trim the black clay flush with the transfer image.

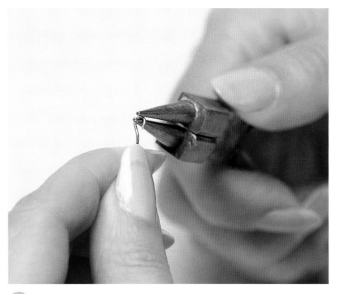

3 Use rosary pliers to bend the straight end of a head-pin into a loop.

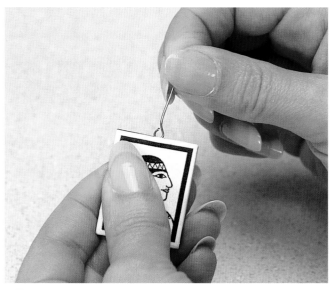

4 Gently insert the loop into the top of the piece, in between the layers. Use a rubber eraser to flatten any bulges made by inserting the headpin.

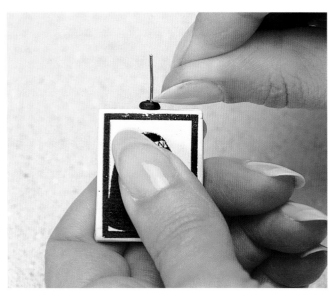

5 Roll a tiny bead of black clay and slip it onto the straight end of the headpin. Slide the bead all the way down the pin and flatten it against the earring with your fingernail. Bake and cool.

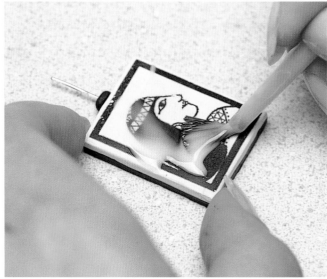

6 Apply a thin layer of TLS to the earring. Bake and cool again, then antique as described on pages 101 and 102, steps 12–14.

7 Using the cutter on the rosary pliers, snip the head-pin to ⅜" (1cm). Bend the end of the headpin into a loop.

8 Re-open the loop by turning it sideways with the tips of the pliers, then slip it through the loop on the French hook earring wire, making sure the earring is facing forward. Close the loop by twisting the pliers in the opposite direction.

Geisha Earrings

Using the geisha mirror image transfers from page 125 and colored pencils, you can create earrings to match the Asian Pendant featured on page 98.

Palette

Earthy

Domed Daisy Pin

The domed shape of this pin is achieved by baking it over an old lightbulb. The batik palette combines a metallic background with translucent canes lined in white, which mimics the resist lines found in hand-dyed batik cloth. Borders around circles are difficult to join without an obvious seam, so several indentations are added to make the border appear continuous.

Palette

Batik

Clay

½ block black ● ¼ block purple + ¼ block blue, marbled (page 18) ● Round petal cane (page 33): purple and translucent wrapped in #1 white, reduced to ¾" (1.9cm) ● Circle cane (page 26): red wrapped in #1 white, reduced to pinhead size ● Veined leaf cane (page 32): green and translucent with #1 white veins, wrapped in #1 white and reduced to ¾" (1.9cm) ● Spiral cane (page 28): #4 blue and #4 translucent wrapped in #2 white, reduced to ¼" (0.6cm)

Tools and Materials

Lightbulb ● Pinback ● Aluminum foil ● Acrylic roller ● Tissue blade ● Craft knife ● 2" (5.1cm) circle cutter ● Metal skewer ● Pasta machine ● Jewelry adhesive (E6000)

1 Run the marbled sheet of clay through the pasta machine on the #5 setting, then run a sheet of black clay through on the same setting. Trim both sheets to 2½" x 2½" (6.4cm x 6.4cm) and set the excess clay from the #5 black sheet aside for use in step 6. Layer the marbled sheet on top of the black sheet. Arrange slices of the round petal cane in a circle to form a daisy and make a flower center with circle cane slices. Fill the rest of the design with veined leaf, circle and spiral canes and flatten with an acrylic roller.

2 Cut a 2" (5.1cm) circle from the design sheet with the circle cutter.

3 Place the design sheet on the end of a lightbulb and smooth it down with your palm to create a dome.

4 Tear off a few inches of aluminum foil and make it into a doughnut shape, as shown.

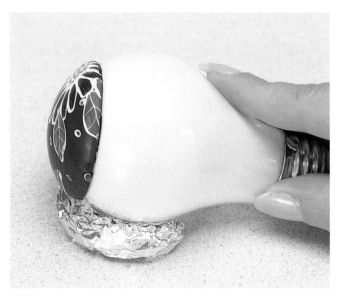

5 Position the lightbulb so that the side is resting on the doughnut of aluminum foil. Bake and cool.

6 Cut out a 2" (5.1cm) circle from the remaining black #5 sheet from step 1 with the circle cutter.

7 Place the baked dome on the #5 black sheet. Roll a black clay snake about ³⁄₁₆" (0.5cm) thick and place it around the dome. Smooth the snake with your fingernail.

8 Make an indentation at the seam of the snake with the side of a metal skewer, then repeat to make decorative indentations around the piece as desired.

9 Smooth the sides by rolling the snake border along your work surface. Bake and cool. Score the back of the pin with a craft knife and adhere the pinback with jewelry adhesive. To further secure the pinback, cover the attached bracket with a pinch of black clay, bake and cool.

Domed Daisy Earrings

To make these earrings, all you have to do is adjust the size of the cutter, border and canes. Reduce the veined leaf and round petal canes to ¼" (0.6cm), reduce the border to ⅛" (0.3cm) and use a 1" (2.5cm) circle cutter to cut out the shapes. Bake and cool, then adhere pierced or clip-on findings, depending on the style you prefer.

Palette

Batik

Fragment Pin

There are always fragments of design sheets left over from other projects, so why not put them to good use? This fun and easy project incorporates fragments into a collage-like pin. The patterned fragments become an abstract element against the deeply textured black clay that surrounds them. And the best part about it is that you're cleaning up your work surface by using the extra clay. Nothing will go to waste, and you will have a beautiful pin to show for it!

Palette

Jewel

Clay

½ block black • Scrap design sheet from Bamboo Pin (page 84)

Tools and Materials

Sticks and Stones texture sheet (Polyform) • Water in spray bottle • Pinback • Acrylic roller • Tissue blade • Scissors • Craft knife • Pasta machine • Jewelry adhesive (E6000) • Cardstock • Fragment Pin template (page 124)

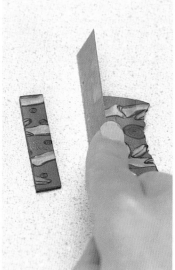

1 Run a sheet of conditioned black clay through the pasta machine on the #5 setting and cut it in half. Set one half aside for use in step 3. Spritz the remaining half with water and lay the texture sheet on top. Impress the sheet into the clay and roll with an acrylic roller. Cut the sheet into three thin strips measuring about ½" x 2¼" (1.3cm x 5.7cm).

2 Run the scrap design sheet through the pasta machine on the #5 setting and cut it into two thin strips measuring about ½" x 2¼" (1.3cm x 5.7cm).

3 Place the strips next to each other, alternating between black and colored, on top of the remaining #5 black sheet. Roll the strips with an acrylic roller to fuse them together. Copy and cut out the template, place it over the sheet and cut out the shape. Bake and cool. Score the back of the pin with a craft knife and adhere a pinback with jewelry adhesive. To further secure the pinback, cover the attached bracket with a pinch of black clay, bake and cool.

Scrap Clay Earrings

These earrings can be made with scrap canes and left-over design sheets from any of the projects in this book. The sizes, shapes, colors and designs demonstrated here are only to give you ideas. Feel free to use any of your leftover canes and design sheets and experiment with different shapes and sizes. If you want to make a pair of earrings to match a pin, bracelet or necklace, just reduce the cane or cut the design sheet to a smaller size before adding the earring findings. This demonstration shows how to make one earring, but I recommend making both at the same time.

Palettes
Tropical and Earthy

Clay

Leaf petal cane (page 34): green and yellow with #2 red veins ● Scrap design sheet from Wearable Vessel (page 88) ● Black clay

Tools and Materials

Headpins ● Jump rings ● Earring findings (pierced or clip-on posts, French hook earring wires, etc.) ● Rubber eraser ● Rosary pliers ● Needle-nose pliers ● Tissue blade ● Craft knife ● 1" (2.5cm) circle cutter ● ³⁄₈" (1cm) circle cutter ● Jewelry adhesive (E6000)

Cane Slice Earrings
Follow these simple steps to make earrings from cane slices. This projects shows earrings made with a veined leaf cane, but any of the other canes will work just as well.

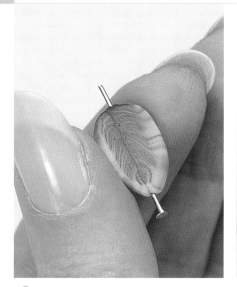  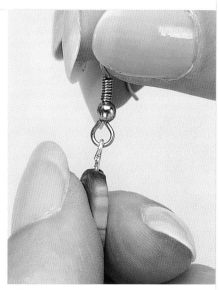

1 Use your tissue blade to cut a thick slice from the cane, then flatten it with a rubber eraser. Insert a headpin through the slice so that the bottom of the slice rests against the head of the pin. Flatten the slice again, then bake and cool with the headpin in place.

2 Trim the headpin to ¼" (0.6cm) and use rosary pliers to bend it into a loop.

3 Open the loop sideways, fasten it to the earring finding, then close the loop.

Geometric Shape Earrings

Save leftover design sheets from your other jewelry pieces to make earrings in any shape you desire. Clay cutters are available in craft stores, and you can also get creative by using tiny cookie cutters or even carving out your own free-form shapes!

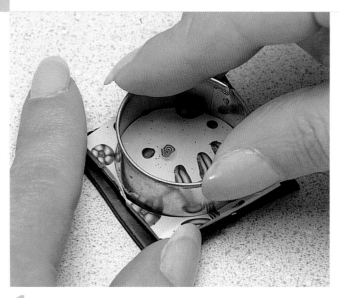

1 Place a scrap design sheet onto a sheet of black clay and cut out a circle with the 1" (2.5cm) circle cutter.

2 To make post earrings, bake and cool the clay circles and score the backs of the baked pieces with a craft knife. Adhere the posts with jewelry adhesive.

3 To make dangle earrings, punch a hole out of the top of the raw clay circle from step 1 with the ⅜" (1cm) circle cutter. Bake and cool.

4 Open a jump ring by twisting the rosary and needle-nose pliers in opposite directions. Thread the jump ring through the hole in the earring, then fasten the dangle finding to the jump ring. Twist the pliers to close.

Mayan Earrings

The Mayan Moon Goddess art in an oval format is transferred onto gold clay and illustrates how the shape of the design can differ from the shape of the earrings.

Palette

Jewel

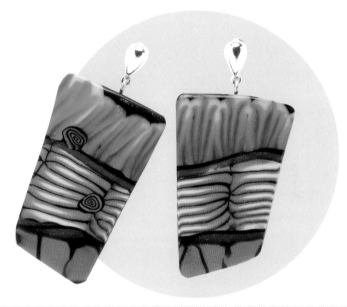

Eclectic Earrings

Scraps from the tropical palette are hand-cut into a pair of earrings whose shape does not match perfectly, for a more eclectic attitude.

Palette

Tropical

Mum Earrings

Thin, wedge-shaped earrings are cut from the patterned sheet of the Chrysanthemum Fan Pin design sheet (page 96).

Palette

Opal

Gallery

These are samples of my original polymer clay jewelry. You will recognize some of the cane designs from the projects. There is a thread of similarity throughout the pieces, whether cane, color or motif, yet all are one-of-a-kind.

Bone-Shaped Bamboo Pin
This is a variation of the Bamboo Pin on page 84, done without a frame and in a bone shape.

Flower Faerie Pendant
This larger faerie is dressed in flower petal and leaf cane slices. They are easy to see on her skirt, but it is only when you look closely that you notice the canes that make up her shoes.

Mini Faerie Pendant
This teeny-tiny faerie pendant illustrates the diversity of using canes. The delicate lace of her dress is made from crackle canes.

Swirl Pendant
Metallic pearl clay, which I used in this mokume gane swirl pendant, seems almost dimensional when sanded and polished.

Free-form Mum Pin

Another variation of the chrysanthemum design, this pin is cut into a more free-form shape by hand.

Daphne Pendant

The portrait on this disc pendant is an actual pencil drawing I did on baked clay, protected by a layer of TLS and framed by cane slices. The beaded bezel and fringe are an exotic complement to the polymer clay disc.

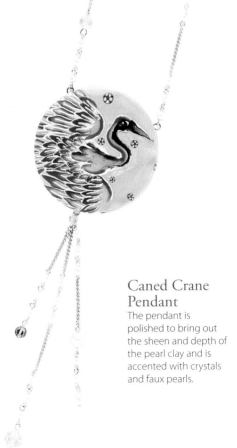

Kimono Pin

This kitschy kimono design uses a smaller version of the daisy motif in a repeated pattern that is meant to mimic fabric. It would look cute as a pendant, as well.

Caned Crane Pendant

The pendant is polished to bring out the sheen and depth of the pearl clay and is accented with crystals and faux pearls.

Templates

Following are patterns for some of the projects in this book. Photocopy them onto cardstock or trace them onto a piece of paper and cut them out as needed. All the templates are shown here at full size.

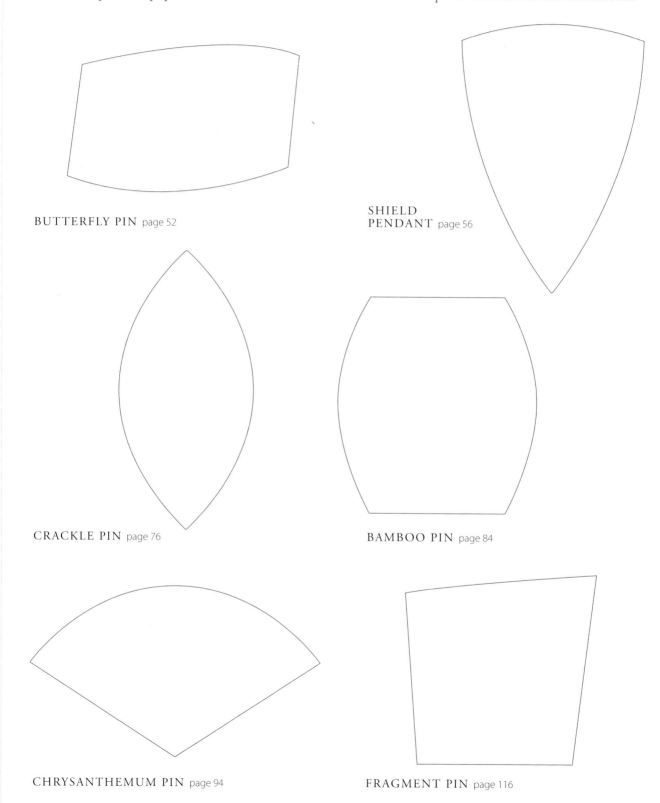

BUTTERFLY PIN page 52

SHIELD
PENDANT page 56

CRACKLE PIN page 76

BAMBOO PIN page 84

CHRYSANTHEMUM PIN page 94

FRAGMENT PIN page 116

Transfer Images

Copy this art for your own use on a toner-based photocopier for transfers
and on a color copier for applied images that will be glued down.

Resources

Most of the supplies in this book are readily available through art and craft stores. If you have difficulty locating any of these materials, here is a list of manufacturers that will be able to direct you to a supplier in your area.

AMACO
14417 West 16th Street
Indianapolis, IN 46222
Phone: 1 (800) 374-1600
Web site: www.amaco.com
Polymer clay, miniature cutters, pasta machines

APPLIANCES.COM
11558 SR 44
Mantua, OH 44255
Phone: 1 (888) 543-8345
Web site: www.appliances.com
Pasta machines

BEADBOX
1290 North Scottsdale Road
Suite 104
Tempe, AZ 85281-1703
Phone: (480) 967-4080
Web site: www.beadbox.com
Findings, beads, pliers

CLAY FACTORY OF ESCONDIDO
P.O. Box #460598
Escondido, CA 92046-0598
Phone: 1 (877) SCULPEY (728-5739)
Web site: www.clayfactoryinc.com
Polymer clay, miniature cutters, tissue blades, mica powders

DOVER BOOKS
31 East 2nd Street
Mineola, NY 11501-3852
Phone: (516) 294-7000
Web site: www.doverpublications.com
Copyright-free art and illustrations

FIRE MOUNTAIN GEMS
One Fire Mountain Way
Grants Pass, OR 97526-2373
Phone: 1 (800) 355-2137
Web site: www.firemountaingems.com
Beads and jewelry-making supplies

NANETTA BANANTO
Web site: www.nanettabananto.com
Jewelry, illustration, paper arts, dolls, beadwork, instruction

NATIONAL POLYMER CLAY GUILD
1350 Beverly Road
McLean, VA 22101
Web site: www.npcg.org
Promotion, education and awareness of polymer clay

GLASS ATTIC
www.glassattic.com
Polymer clay information and techniques

POLYFORM PRODUCTS
1905 Estes Avenue
Elk Grove Village, IL 60007
Phone: (847) 427-0020
Web site: www.sculpey.com
Polymer clay, texture sheets, tissue blades, molds, online projects (check out mine!)

RIO GRANDE
7500 Bluewater Road NW
Albuquerque, NM 87121-1962
Phone: 1 (800) 545-6566
Web site: www.riogrande.com
Jewelry findings, beads, rosary pliers

UNIEK
805 Uniek Drive
Waunakee, WI 53597-0457
Phone: 1 (800) 248-6435 ext. 300
Web site: www.uniek.com
Nylon craft cord

Index

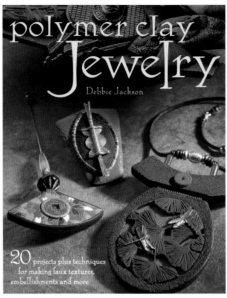

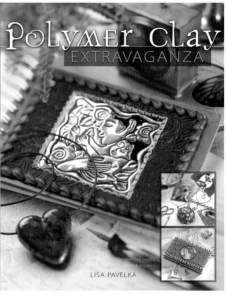

POLYMER CLAY JEWELRY
By Debbie Jackson

Learn to create 20 gorgeous projects with an array of polymer clay and jewelry making techniques. Debbie Jackson shows you how to use embellishments, textures, liquid polymer clay and canes to create one-of-a-kind pieces that will dazzle your friends and loved ones.
ISBN 1-58180-513-6, pb, 128 pages, #32873-K

POLYMER CLAY EXTRAVAGANZA
By Lisa Pavelka

Fast and fun, this book features 20 dazzling projects that combine easy polymer clay techniques with a variety of accessible mediums, including mosaic, wire stamping, foiling, millefiore, caning and metal embossing. Step-by-step instructions, full color photos and a section for beginners guarantees success. This unique guide also includes an inspiring idea gallery that encourages crafters to expand their creativity and develop original pieces of their own.
ISBN 1-58180-188-2, pb, 128 pages, #31960-K

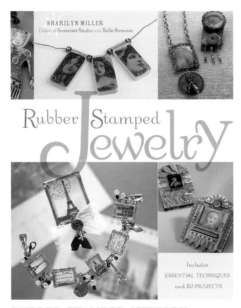

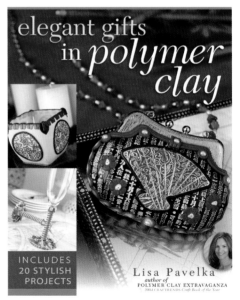

RUBBER STAMPED JEWELRY
By Sharilyn Miller

This book combines the self-expressive qualities of rubber stamping with the elegance of jewelry making. Through easy-to-follow instructions and beautiful full-color photos, Sharilyn Miller provides all the invaluable tips and techniques you need to create earrings, necklaces, bracelets and brooches using a wide array of materials like fabric, shrink plastic and more. The book also includes 20 projects from the author and contributing artists.
ISBN 1-58180-384-2, pb, 128 pages, #32415-K

ELEGANT GIFTS IN POLYMER CLAY
By Lisa Pavelka

Award-winning author Lisa Pavelka presents exciting techniques for creating 20 simple polymer clay gift items that are elegant works of art, including a picture frame, beaded pendant and more.
ISBN 1-58180-571-3, pb, 128 pages, #33028-K